What Others Are Saying About Pastor Kynan Bridges and *Defeating Darkness*…

Defeating Darkness exhorts us to rise up from defeat and to live according to the fullness of blessings in Christ Jesus. In this book, Kynan Bridges has caught hold of a precious truth that every believer needs to hear and walk out in daily life. Read the biblical truth in its pages, allow the Word to transform your thinking, and begin to allow God to turn your life into what He meant it to be. This fresh, powerful read will help you lay hold of the riches of glory in Christ Jesus and enable you to walk in His victory.

—Aliss Cresswell
Codirector, MorningStar Europe

In *Defeating Darkness: Spiritual Warfare for Everyday Battles*, Pastor Kynan Bridges shares powerful spiritual insights that will help the body of Christ step into possessing a place of authority over the plans and schemes of the enemy. You will grow by leaps and bounds as you learn how to sharpen the sword of the Spirit and take dominion over negative thoughts, strongholds, and sources of oppression. Be trained to walk in your God-given rights as a believer. Become the head, and stop allowing the enemy to steal your destiny. Be a victor instead of becoming a victim as you practice what you glean from Kynan's anointed writing.

—Dr. Barbie L. Breathitt
Breath of the Spirit Ministries
Author, *Dream Seer*, *Dream Interpreter*, *Gateway to the Seer Realm*, and *Dream Encounters*

Prophetic voices are rising up, pronouncing a third Great Awakening, but pushing back the darkness demands a revelation of our authority in Christ. In his book *Defeating Darkness*, Kynan Bridges offers a fresh perspective on an ancient truth about the believer's position of power in a raging spiritual war. He equips you to stand up and fight for the promises of God for your life, your city, and your nation.

—*Jennifer LeClaire*
Author, *The Spiritual Warrior's Guide to Defeating Jezebel*
Senior Leader, Awakening House of Prayer,
Ft. Lauderdale, Florida

Kynan Bridges stirs up a passion and hunger within the heart of the believer to long for and see the glory of God! He prepares the body of Christ to get ready to see our all-powerful God work in our lives and manifest His glory and kingdom.

—*Dr. Jeremy Lopez*
CEO, IdentityNetwork.net

Pastor Kynan Bridges has done it again! The revelation of the Word that he shares will give you keys to mighty kingdom realities. As you apply the revelations he teaches, you will find the power of God to literally erase the borders of the impossible. And as you follow the truths that Pastor Bridges presents, you will deepen your relationship with the Father and the Son and, in the process, discover your authority to disarm, defeat, and demolish the powers of darkness! You have been given authority over the spirits of darkness so that souls might be saved, sick bodies might be healed, and people's lives might be transformed for the glory of God.

—*Pastor Tony Kemp*
Tony Kemp Ministries, Inc.

One of the saddest situations ever encountered is a person who actually possesses great wealth but doesn't have knowledge of it. Most of us have heard of elderly people who died in poverty, only to have it revealed upon their death that they actually possessed a bank account containing more than a million dollars, yet never accessed it because they didn't know about it. Likewise, many believers have no idea of the authority they possess as ambassadors of Jesus Christ on the earth; consequently, they allow the enemy to bully them and control their lives. But no more! If you read and apply the revelation knowledge Kynan Bridges imparts in *Defeating Darkness*, demons and spiritual enemies will never be able to bully you again. Kynan does a masterful job of helping you understand exactly what authority has been given to you and showing you, practically, how you can use that authority. Don't waste another day allowing the enemy to torment or hold you in bondage. Pick up this book, read it, and apply the truths within. Your life will never be the same!

—*Craig Hill*
Founder, Family Foundations International
www.familyfoundations.com

DEFEATING DARKNESS

SPIRITUAL WARFARE FOR
EVERYDAY BATTLES

KYNAN BRIDGES

Whitaker House

Unless otherwise indicated, all Scripture quotations are taken from the King James Version of the Holy Bible. Scripture quotation marked (NASB) is taken from the updated *New American Standard Bible*®, NASB®, © 1960, 1962, 1963, 1968, 1971, 1972, 1973, 1975, 1977, 1995 by The Lockman Foundation. Used by permission. (www.Lockman.org). Scripture quotation marked (AMP) is taken from *The Amplified*® *Bible*, © 1954, 1958, 1962, 1964, 1965, 1987 by The Lockman Foundation. Used by permission. (www.Lockman.org).

Boldface type in the Scripture quotations indicates the author's emphasis.

Definitions of Hebrew and Greek words are taken from *The New Strong's Exhaustive Concordance of the Bible* (© 1990, Thomas Nelson Publishers. Used by permission. All rights reserved.).

Dictionary definitions are taken from either *Merriam-Webster's 11th Collegiate Dictionary*, electronic version, © 2013, or the *OxfordDictionaries.com*, Oxford University Press, © 2014.

DEFEATING DARKNESS
Spiritual Warfare for Everyday Battles
(Previously published under the title *Kingdom Authority*)

Kynan Bridges Ministries, Inc.
P. O. Box 159
Ruskin, FL 33575
www.kynanbridges.com

ISBN: 979-8-88769-463-4
eBook ISBN: 979-8-88769-464-1
Printed in the United States of America
© 2025 by Kynan Bridges

Whitaker House
1030 Hunt Valley Circle
New Kensington, PA 15068
www.whitakerhouse.com

Library of Congress Control Number: 2025910867

No part of this book may be reproduced or transmitted in any form or by any means, electronic or mechanical—including photocopying, recording, or by any information storage and retrieval system—without permission in writing from the publisher. Please direct your inquiries to permissionseditor@whitakerhouse.com.

1 2 3 4 5 6 7 8 9 10 11 ɯ 32 31 30 29 28 27 26 25

DEDICATION

I dedicate this book to the Lord Jesus Christ, the King of Kings and Lord of Lords.

I also dedicate it to Gloria Bridges—my lovely and virtuous wife, the mother of my five beautiful children (Ella, Naomi, Isaac, Israel, and Anna), and my number one supporter in life and ministry. I love you more than words can express.

And to my church family (Grace & Peace Global Fellowship), who have been instrumental in praying for and supporting this project—God bless you!

ACKNOWLEDGMENTS

First of all, I want to acknowledge my precious Lord Jesus Christ. It is through Him that I am able to write this book and all the others I have authored.

To my lovely wife, Gloria—I love and appreciate you for who you area and all that you do on a daily basis.

To my ministerial staff at Kynan Bridges Ministries, Inc., especially my staff editor, Isheka Harrison—thank you!

To my parents, James and Juanita Bridges—I honor you.

To Whitaker House Publishers—thank you for believing in me and helping to release this message to the body of Christ. Special thanks to the production and editorial teams, including Christine Whitaker, Courtney Hartzel, and Don Milam, to name a few.

I also want to take a moment and acknowledge some of the great men and women of the faith who have impacted my life and ministry in a positive way, either directly or indirectly: Pastor Wayne C. Thompson, Dr. Mark Chironna, Derek Prince, Smith Wigglesworth, John G. Lake, Oswald Chambers, John Wesley, Jack Coe, Oral Roberts, Kathryn Kuhlman, R. W. Schambach, Kenneth E. Hagin, Dr. T. L. Osborn, Dr. Martin Luther King Jr., Heidi

Baker, Bill Johnson, Randy Clark, Mahesh and Bonnie Chavda, Hank and Brenda Kunneman, Apostle Guillermo Maldonado, Sid Roth, Rabbi Jonathan Bernis, Dr. Cindy Trimm, Apostle Charles Ndifon, Charles and Frances Hunter, Joan Hunter, Pastor Marlin D. Harris, Dr. E. V. Hill, Dr. Barbie Breathitt, Mike Bickle, Pastor Andre Mitchell, Apostle Mark T. Jones, Marilyn Hickey, Pastor Tony Kemp, John Loren Sandford, Dr. T. L. Lowery, Dr. Douglas Wingate, Benny Hinn, evangelist Reinhard Bonnke, and Dr. Rodney Howard-Browne. Thank you for your service and gift to the body of Christ.

God bless you!

CONTENTS

Foreword by Sid Roth 13
Preface 16
Introduction 18
  1. Understanding Authority 21
  2. Knowing Your Rights 32
  3. Who Do You Think You Are? 47
  4. Bedtime Stories 58
  5. Darkness Defined 79
  6. Exposing the Enemy 94
  7. Called to Conquer 114
  8. Dressed for Battle 126
  9. Taking Dominion 136
 10. The Position of Power 146
 11. Breaking Demonic Strongholds 158
 12. Disrupting the Enemy's Patterns 172
 13. The Shield of Faith 184
 14. Stand and Fight! 193
About the Author 205

FOREWORD

Jesus came down with them and stood on a level place; and there was a large crowd of His disciples, and a great throng of people from all Judea and Jerusalem...who had come to hear Him and to be healed of their diseases; and those who were troubled with unclean spirits were being cured. And all the people were trying to touch Him, for power was coming from Him and healing them all.
—Luke 6:17–19 (NASB)

When I was thirty years old, I faced a crisis. I had taken a course in Eastern meditation and knew I was demonized. Since I was Jewish, I did not know where to turn. If I went to my parents or to my rabbi, the best they could do would be to send me to a psychiatrist. No psychiatrist could get rid of these demons. I wish I'd had a book like *Defeating Darkness*, by my friend Kynan Bridges. But a few brave Christians told me there was a greater power in the name of Jesus than in all the demons in hell. With seemingly my last ounce of strength, I cried out, "Jesus, help!" Then I virtually gave up, not caring whether I ever woke up again, because life had become unbearable. I fell into a deep sleep, totally exhausted.

The next morning, I awoke to a presence in my room that felt like liquid love. I immediately knew Jesus was my Messiah and that I never wanted to be separated from His love again. And the demons were not able to coexist with the love of God. They immediately fled!

But then, several months later, they came back. I did not know what to do. Although I had been sovereignly saved and delivered, I had not been trained on how to take dominion over the powers of darkness. Eventually, I learned how—the hard way. Had I had this book in my hands, I could have avoided years of struggling with the enemy. *Defeating Darkness* is a vital end-time mentoring tool.

Kynan is a God-anointed teacher, and, even better, he teaches from experience rather than theory. Years ago, I watched a secular TV interview featuring a priest who was in charge of the deliverance ministry for the Catholic Church. It was obvious to me that he knew very little about deliverance. And he is not alone. Most of the body of the Messiah is woefully ignorant of Satan's strategies.

One third of Jesus' ministry involved casting out evil spirits from people. If a sickness is caused by an evil spirit, healing will not happen until the evil spirit has been cast out. Sometimes, Jesus would pray for healing; sometimes, He would pray for deliverance. We need to be equipped for both types of ministries.

We also must be prepared to help those who are tormented by nightmares, anxiety attacks, chronic fear, poverty, lust, and addictions to such things as pornography, drugs, alcohol, and depression. We must have answers.

There is a dire lack of information about deliverance in the church. There is also rampant fear of the devil and ignorance of our authority as believers. All of the above is instigated by the evil spirits themselves.

A great prophet who is now in heaven told me there would come a time when millions of young people would be flooded with demons. The media, drugs, the education system, New Age philosophy, and low standards of morality are all opening doors to the demonic. He told me the reason young people are being targeted is because God is about to pour out His Spirit on them and cause them to be leaders in the next revival. He said many of these young people will be radically saved, and almost all will need deliverance.

We are about to experience the greatest revival in history. God has put this book in your hands for such a time as this, to set the captives free!

—*Sid Roth*
Host, *It's Supernatural!* television show

PREFACE

Ever since I was a young boy, I understood that I was not alone in this world. At an early age, I had a profound awareness of God's presence, but I was equally aware of such a thing called "darkness." When I rededicated my life to Jesus in 1996, I encountered this darkness firsthand. For several months, I was tormented by nightmares, demonic attacks in my sleep, and the spirit of fear. Little did I know that satanic assaults on the mind and body were not unique to me. Countless people in the church have faced battles with the realm of darkness, yet many of them remain silent.

One night, on the verge of being suffocated to death in my sleep, I called on the only name that I knew to call upon—the name of Jesus. Instantly, I was set free from the tyrannical grip of the devil. It was in that moment that I realized I had authority over the enemy. I came to see that the name of Jesus was more than a word used casually in Sunday school; it was the embodiment of the sovereign power of the kingdom of God.

Since that day, I have been on a crusade to liberate God's people from the demonic strongholds of fear, depression, lust, sickness, poverty, and bondage. Throughout my life and ministry, I have witnessed countless people being delivered and radically transformed by the power of Jesus.

As you read this book, you will come to realize that you, too—as a believer—have authority over the devil. From the pages of this book, you will gain deep biblical insight into the power that you possess as a child of God. You will discover how to utilize the Word of God and the name of Jesus to gain victory over the enemy and take dominion over the powers of darkness. Your life will never be the same!

—Pastor Kynan Bridges

INTRODUCTION

"Pastor, pray for me! I feel like I am under attack!" This statement has been repeated countless times by millions of people all around the world. Every day, I receive hundreds of messages in my e-mail inbox from individuals requesting help finding freedom from some pervasive area of bondage or oppression in their lives. Why is this the case? I believe that it has to do with the fact that we are living in the last days.

That this is more than a simple eschatological (end-times) statement—it is a spiritual reality. Regardless of your theological and eschatological beliefs, you will find it difficult to deny that demonic activity has reached an all-time high. I believe the reason for this is very simple: The devil knows he has a short time to wait until his ultimate defeat. (See Revelation 12:12.) And I believe that this is a good sign. "What do you mean by that?" you ask. The Bible tells us, *"Where sin abounded, grace did much more abound"* (Romans 5:20). In the midst of challenges, difficulties, and intense spiritual warfare, God is releasing His supernatural power for healing, breakthrough, and deliverance like never before. In fact, I believe that we are entering into the greatest time the church has ever seen. As evil increases in the earth, so too the power to overcome that evil will also increase.

The reason I wrote this book was to equip believers to take up their spiritual weapons in order to resist the enemy's activity in their lives. It is time for the body of Christ to walk in the fullness of her true identity. God has no question as to who we are, but many believers in the church have seemed to abandon their true identity. This is about to change!

When I was a young boy, Satan attacked me in a horrific way. His intent was to instill fear in my heart so that I would not commit fully to the ministry to which God had called me. Unfortunately for the devil, he picked a fight with the wrong person. I have never been a good victim. Instead of terrifying me, he merely annoyed me. As a friend of mine once said, "Your greatest annoyance is your greatest anointing!" What Satan meant to torment and oppress me became the catalyst for my ministry of healing and deliverance. Ever since then, it has been my ardent quest to see the people of God liberated from the oppression of the enemy and walking in their supernatural inheritance.

Whether you have been battling with lustful thoughts, wrestling with addiction, or tormented by fear and anxiety, the information in this book will empower you to walk in the kingdom authority you have been destined for. The kingdom keys contained herein, when fully embraced, will cause you to experience total freedom from demonic oppression. Contrary to what you may have thought, you don't have to live in bondage ever again. God envisions His church as a powerful spiritual organism, capable of bringing change and transformation to the world around it! He sees a church that drives out demonic forces from people, atmospheres, territories, and nations. He sees a church that is fully engaged in its kingdom mandate to teach and disciple the nations, according to Matthew 28:19.

When I first became a Christian, no one taught me about spiritual warfare; and so, when I was ravaged by demonic attacks in the form of nightmares, physical oppression, fear, and lust, I didn't know what to do. Thanks be to God for revealing to me how to win the battle against the forces of darkness and how to walk in the authority of Jesus! And praise be to Him for the privilege of sharing this information with the body of Christ.

Many books that I have read on this topic focus on the demonic, but they fail to recognize the identity and the authority of the believer as the greatest weapon of our warfare. Simply put, knowing who we are and whose we are is the key to winning the battle against the devil.

In this book, my goal is to demystify the subject of spiritual warfare (and the supernatural, in general), making it easy to understand and comprehend from a biblical and revelatory perspective. It is written in such a way that a layperson can understand, yet the content is potent enough for a pastor, a prophet, or an intercessory minister to implement.

The authority of the believer, combined with strategic spiritual warfare and a foundation of faith, acts as a threefold cord essential to winning spiritual battles against such woes as depression, chronic sickness, anxiety, fear, bitterness, perversion, rejection, and demonic strongholds.

My ultimate prayer is that you will be encouraged by the truths I am about to share with you. Freedom is not as far away as you have assumed. Not only are you going to experience supernatural freedom and breakthrough, but, after reading this book, you will also be in a position to minister deliverance to friends, family members, and other loved ones.

UNDERSTANDING AUTHORITY

Behold, I give unto you power to tread on serpents and scorpions, and over all the power of the enemy: and nothing shall by any means hurt you.
—Luke 10:19

One of my favorite mythical tales is the ancient Greek legend of Helen of Troy. Referenced in Homer's *Odyssey*, the story tells of a decade-long battle between the Greeks and the Trojans, or the people of Troy. The city of Troy was known for its impenetrable walls and for the military might of its army. No other army could prevail against the Trojans.

Less powerful than the Trojans, the Greeks had to resort to deception and subterfuge in order to defeat their enemy. They constructed a wooden horse, in which they hid an elite force of men, and presented it to the king of Troy as a gift meant to symbolize the Greeks' humility. While the Greek army pretended to sail away, the Trojans brought the horse within their gates in order to celebrate their defeat of the Greeks. Little did they know that the horse was filled with soldiers waiting to burst out, kill the Trojans from within their own gates, and then open the doors to the rest of the Greek army, secretly waiting just outside the city walls.

Mythical though it is, this tale paints a very vivid picture of the current state of the body of Christ. The authority that Christ has given us is literally impenetrable, but there are countless people who have allowed the "Trojan horse" of fear, doubt, and unbelief to rob them of the authority that is rightfully theirs in Christ. The truth is that Satan doesn't stand a chance against the body of Christ; but if he can keep us ignorant of his evil agenda, we will unknowingly invite him in to wreak havoc in our lives.

This very situation is taking place throughout the church today. Millions of people are being tormented by nightmares, anxiety attacks, chronic fears, poverty, lust, addictions, and depression. These are nothing more than Trojan horses, used by the enemy to open the door to bondage in our lives.

Beloved, there is a war going on. This is a struggle between good and evil, light and darkness. This war is evident from the evil we see all around us. The way you respond to this spiritual war will determine whether you experience "life more abundantly," as Jesus promised us (see John 10:10), or "life more defeated." You must remember, the devil is not interested in simply attacking your mind, emotions, or body; he desires to completely conquer your life. The question remains: What are you going to do about it? That's right—you have a role to fulfill. Are you going to simply roll over and play dead, while the devil lays siege to your ministry, marriage, mind, finances, or other areas of your life?

I am here to announce to you that the time of your captivity is over! As you read this book, God is going to open your eyes to a new and wonderful reality—a reality where you walk in victory for the rest of your life. Are you ready?

Early Impressions of Authority

What is authority? When I hear that word, I often think of the school resource officers I grew up fearing. Employed by the board of education, these officers were responsible for monitoring the hallways and keeping the peace inside the four walls of the middle school that I attended. They always had a very serious look on their faces and often carried a gun at their waist. Every now and then, a student would attempt to challenge one of the resource officers—never a pretty sight.

Whenever this happened, as I watched the officer forcefully escort the rebellious student to in-school suspension, I had a glimpse of authority. I was always struck by the fact that there was no way to get around the officer's authority because he was backed by the entire board of education of the county. To challenge the officer was to challenge the entire board of education. The only way that a student might have prevailed against the officer would have been to convince him or her to resign his or her authority or to somehow fall out of right standing with the board and get fired as a result.

Through my observations of these officers and the role they played in enforcing the rules, I believe God was trying to teach me a valuable lesson that would be useful for the rest of my life and ministry.

We Have Authority Over the Enemy!

As a pastor, I have witnessed the defeat and despair that plague thousands of believers. Many are ignorant concerning the spiritual nature of the darkness waging war against them, and countless more are unaware of the authority that they possess, as children of God, to deal with this darkness.

When God made the first man, Adam, in the garden of Eden, He gave him inherent authority. This authority was connected to its heavenly source: Almighty God. As long as Adam was in right standing with his heavenly Father, everything in the garden was made subject to him.

In a sense, Adam was the "resource officer" of the earth. He was entrusted with maintaining order and balance in the garden. This job included "dressing" and "keeping" the garden environment. (See Genesis 2:15.) In that verse, the word "*dress*" comes from the Hebrew word `abad, which means "to serve," "to labor," or "to work." God gave Adam a divine assignment. He also told him to "keep" the garden. In Genesis 2:15, the word "*keep*" comes from the Hebrew word *shâmar*, which means to "keep," "regard," "watch," "observe," and "protect." Adam was the literal guard, or warden, of the garden of Eden.

God granted Adam authority to carry out a specific assignment, and that assignment was to keep order and balance on the earth. Again, what is authority? Authority is the right to act in a specified way, delegated from one person or organization to another. In this case, authority was delegated from God to man. And this authority was never meant to function independently of the source from which it had been delegated. God commissioned Adam to represent Him in the earthly realm. But the moment Adam ate of the Tree of Knowledge of Good and Evil, he abdicated his authority and surrendered his badge of delegation to the evil one.

As a result of man's disobedience against God, mankind forfeited his legal right to rule and reign on the earth. In a single moment, humankind came under the jurisdiction of Satan, and chaos and disorder ensued. Consequently, mankind was made subject to sickness, oppression, fear, and even death. Adam's sin opened the door to spiritual darkness. This is the reason why evil is so pervasive across the globe today! The good news is that, two thousand years ago, God came to the earth as a Man, suffered on a cross, died, and rose again in order to defeat the devil. By His sacrificial act, He took back from Satan the authority that He had originally granted to the sons of men.

The Bible says, *"For the Son of man is come to seek and to save that which was lost"* (Luke 19:10). What did Jesus come to earth to seek and to save? I believe that He came not only to restore the house of Israel to God but also to restore the entire human race to a position of authority over the enemy. In fact, God, through His Son Jesus, has created in Him an entirely new race of people. (See 2 Corinthians 5:17.) Jesus told His disciples, *"Behold, I give unto you power to tread on serpents and scorpions, and over all the power of the enemy: and nothing shall by any means hurt you"* (Luke 10:19). The word *"power"* in this verse comes from the Greek word *exousia*, which refers to the power of authority, the power of rule or government, or the liberty to do as one chooses. Jesus gave to His disciples the authority to rule over and govern the devil and all his evil powers. And this authority is what gave the disciples—and what gives us today—the legal right to rebuke evil spirits, cast out devils, heal the sick, and otherwise subjugate the devil and his demons.

WE HAVE BEEN GIVEN AUTHORITY OVER DEMONIC SPIRITS, SICKNESS, AND ALL THE POWERS OF DARKNESS.

The questions remain: What are the implications of this kind of authority? How can we use this authority to exercise spiritual rule over the powers of darkness? Is the church utilizing the measure of authority it has been given in Christ? The answers to these questions will determine whether you and I live in victory or in defeat. The reality is that many people are ignorant of the authority they have been given in Christ, and countless more have assumed the fragile posture of powerless religion.

If you are like me, you were probably taught, either explicitly or implicitly, to be afraid of the enemy. The devil was painted as a sort of bogeyman or another type of scary figure that you were supposed to fear and avoid. I can even remember people warning me, for example, "Don't say that—the devil will hear you!"

This and similar sentiments are rooted in fear, and the Bible says that *"fear hath torment"* (1 John 4:18). That kind of thinking is unbiblical and ultimately unproductive because it does not bring victory. But the moment you discover the secret to biblical authority, the devil will be trembling in his boots. The truth is, you can begin living a life of joy, peace, and victory—starting right now.

Seated in Heavenly Places

We have more authority over the enemy than we often realize. Once we embrace this God-given authority in Christ, the enemy will be more afraid of us than we are of him.

In his letter to the Ephesians, the apostle Paul captures the following great truth:

> *But God, who is rich in mercy, for his great love wherewith he loved us, even when we were dead in sins, hath quickened us together with Christ, (by grace ye are saved;) and hath raised us up together, and made us sit together in heavenly places in Christ Jesus.* (Ephesians 2:4–6)

Did you know that you are seated with Christ in heavenly places? What does this really mean? The phrase *"sit together"* comes from the Greek word *sugkathizō*, which means "to place together," "to cause to sit down together." It refers to an act of benevolence whereby a king or other ruler extends his kingdom to friends, family, and dignitaries as an expression of equality or co-authority. To us, it means that you and I possess the same authority that Jesus Christ has. *Really?* you may think. *Why?*

It is certainly amazing that God has extended His kingdom to us, through Jesus Christ, and has caused us to be joint-heirs with Jesus. (See Romans 8:17.) How does this authority affect us on a daily basis? It means that we don't have to give in to the devil ever again. It means that anxiety, depression, fear, and other types of torment no longer have the legal right to control us. It means that we can bind the evil one and, like the middle school resource officers, carry him to "in-school suspension."

Jesus has anointed us as "spiritual resource officers" in the earthly realm. He took the keys from Satan and gave them back to the church. So, what's the problem? It's very simple: Ignorance! It is impossible to exercise authority that you don't know you possess. The Bible makes it clear that a lack of knowledge is dangerous. In the book of Hosea, God makes the following statement:

> *My people are destroyed for lack of knowledge: because thou hast rejected knowledge, I will also reject thee, that thou shalt be no priest to me: seeing thou hast forgotten the law of thy God, I will also forget thy children.* (Hosea 4:6)

This sobering passage of Scripture has revolutionized my life. Contrary to what is commonly said, what you don't know *can* hurt you.

You Are More Powerful than You Know

One day, while I was meditating on God's Word and praying, I experienced an open vision in which I saw a large angelic being. He stood between ten and fifteen feet tall and was dressed in gold chain mail with a solid gold breastplate covering his chest. This angelic being also wore a huge golden crown upon his head and had a gold sword attached to his waist belt. He was so massive that his very presence was intimidating. His chest spanned about six feet, and each of his legs was the width of a tree trunk. I remember saying, "Lord, this must be a powerful archangel!" To this, the Lord responded, "Son, that is not an angel; that is you in the spiritual realm."

This revelation was absolutely amazing! I realized that we, the children of God, are spiritual giants from His vantage point. Thinking more about it, I remembered that the Bible calls us "kings and priests":

> Jesus Christ...is the faithful witness, and the first begotten of the dead, and the **prince of the kings** of the earth. Unto him that loved us, and washed us from our sins in his own blood, and hath **made us kings and priests** unto God and his Father; to him be glory and dominion for ever and ever. Amen. (Revelation 1:5–6)

In the spiritual realm, we are not a bunch of weak and feeble paupers—we are mighty kings, endowed with the very authority of the Lord Jesus Himself. The problem is that most of us don't realize the magnitude of the authority we possess. In the vision I just described, God was revealing to me my true identity in His kingdom. And He wants to reveal the same thing to you right now. He wants all of us to know that we are well equipped to withstand the enemy and anything that he might attempt to bring against us.

Simply put: You are more powerful than you know! Yet your power is not self-generated; rather, it emanates from the One who resides in you—the One who is far greater than he who rules the dark realms of this world. (See 1 John 4:4.)

Twenty years ago, I was completely ignorant of the person God eventually revealed to me in that open vision. As a result of my ignorance, I allowed the enemy to buffet me in many areas of my life. I didn't know that one swing of the sword of the Spirit (see Ephesians 6:17) could decapitate the devil and completely disable his demonic activity in my life. The moment I caught this revelation was the moment my life took a supernatural turn.

God's Kingdom Revealed

And lead us not into temptation, but deliver us from evil: for thine is the kingdom, and the power, and the glory, for ever. Amen. (Matthew 6:13)

When speaking of authority, it is important to understand where our authority comes from. God's kingdom is the focal point and centerpiece for the authority of the believer. The more we understand the kingdom of God, the more we will understand spiritual authority, and the more we will be in a position to exercise that authority over the enemy.

What is the kingdom of God? The word *"kingdom,"* as used in Matthew 6:13, is derived from the Greek word *basileia*, which refers to royal power, kingship, dominion, and rule. It is the right or authority to rule over or govern a kingdom. Simply put, the kingdom of God is the government and rule of God in heaven and on earth. It is God's domain of authority—a domain that has no boundaries.

As citizens of God's kingdom, we have been granted the power to rule and reign on the earth. Our ultimate rule and reign will come at the end of this age, when we will reign with Christ on the earth (see, for example, 2 Timothy 2:12; Revelation 20:6); but God has also given us the right to reign in the spiritual realm *here* and *now*. We exercise this spiritual kingship by taking authority over the forces of darkness (i.e., demonic spirits, sickness, and oppression).

Not only are we citizens of God's kingdom, but His kingdom lives in us. Jesus told His disciples—and He tells us today—*"Behold, the kingdom of God is within you"* (Luke 17:21). Did you know that the kingdom of God is on the inside of you? And do you know what that means? It means that you carry the government of God on the inside of you—a government that is greater than all the powers of darkness combined.

GOD DESIRES TO MANIFEST HIS KINGDOM IN US AND THROUGH US. THIS KINGDOM AUTHORITY EMPOWERS US TO LIVE IN VICTORY OVER THE ENEMY.

The kingdom of God within you, and the power it imparts, gives you the ability to drive out demons, addictions, sickness, and any other force that runs counter to the kingdom. Unfortunately, there are many Christians who are unfamiliar with the kingdom of God. They don't know that they carry God's authority on the inside of them. As a result, they allow Satan to operate illegally in their lives.

God wants you to know that, just like the man He revealed to me in my vision of the angelic-looking being, you are well equipped and able to walk in victory. However, you can exercise your kingdom authority only to the degree that you are submitted to the authority of God in your life. If you want to overcome the powers of darkness and win the spiritual battles that you face, then you must first learn to submit to God and to His government.

So many people are being oppressed by the devil because they refuse to subject themselves to God's government (i.e., God's will; His way of doing things). There is such a thing called "kingdom culture." A culture is simply the beliefs, customs, and ways of life that govern a particular society. What is the culture of God's kingdom? Paul tells us succinctly in Romans 14:17, *"The kingdom of God is…righteousness, and peace, and joy in the Holy Ghost."*

When we submit to the kingdom culture—to God's way of doing things—we will manifest His authority, power, and glory in every area of our lives.

As we progress through this book, I will lead you in a deliverance prayer at the end of every chapter. Silently or out loud, pray with me right now:

Deliverance Prayer

Father, I thank You for Your power and authority. I thank You that Your Word is the final authority in my life and that, through Your Word, I have been equipped to release Your kingdom on the earth. Your Word says, *"Behold, I give unto you power to tread on serpents and scorpions, and over all the power of the enemy: and nothing shall by any means hurt you."* Therefore, I declare that I have authority over the enemy. No scheme, trap, or device of Satan shall prevail against me, in Jesus' name.

Today, I take my place as a divine resource officer in the earthly realm. Any evil or malevolent force working in my atmosphere must come under the dominion of the name of Jesus and the subduing power of the Holy Spirit. I receive supernatural strength and power in my inner being to walk out the fullness of the authority I have been given in Christ. I declare that I will never again live in subservience to fear, anxiety, depression, or rejection.

Thank You, Lord, for my freedom, deliverance, and breakthrough. I take dominion over all forms of oppression, sickness, and disease, according to the Word of God. Hallelujah! I stand victorious over all the power of the enemy in the matchless name of Jesus Christ, in whose name I pray. Amen!

KNOWING YOUR RIGHTS

Blessed be the God and Father of our Lord Jesus Christ, who hath blessed us with all spiritual blessings in heavenly places in Christ.
—Ephesians 1:3

We the People of the United States, in Order to form a more perfect Union, establish Justice, insure domestic Tranquility, provide for the common defense, promote the general Welfare, and secure the Blessings of Liberty to ourselves and our Posterity, do ordain and establish this Constitution for the United States of America." This sentence constitutes the Preamble to the United States Constitution, drafted in 1787 and ratified between 1789 and 1790. This Constitution was written to ensure the freedom of America as a nation-state and to protect its citizens and political officials from tyrannical rule. Along with the Bill of Rights, the Constitution outlines the rights and privileges of every citizen. To know your constitutional rights is to know your citizenship benefits.

In a similar way, God has formed in Himself a "more perfect union"—a band of brothers and sisters called out of darkness into

His marvelous light, united in Christ Jesus. "We the People" of the kingdom of God have been bought with the precious blood of the Lamb and made citizens of a new nation—a nation of kings and priests—called together to pursue life and liberty. Yet many people in the body of Christ have come under the tyrannical rule of Satan, whether knowingly or unknowingly, because they have long been ignorant of their "constitutional rights." These rights are not mere statements of convenience but declarations of law. If it is important to know the terms set forth in the constitution of the nation in which you live, how much more the "spiritual constitution" of the kingdom of God!

What is the constitution of the kingdom? It's the Word of God! In His Word—the holy Bible—we learn who we are and what we have the right to enjoy under the new covenant, which has been signed and ratified by the blood of Jesus. God has given us His Word as the righteous standard by which we are governed, protected, and blessed.

The Bible says that we have been blessed with *"all spiritual blessings in heavenly places in Christ"* (Ephesians 1:3). What does that mean? The apostle Paul uses the Greek word *eulogia*, which means "fine speaking"—praise, or an oral blessing or laudation. This term also refers to the birthright, a common practice in Jewish culture from Bible times until today. In the Hebraic tradition, a Jewish father would entrust his entire estate to his eldest son. This transaction involved speaking forth an oral blessing that set in motion spiritual forces and literally shaped the destiny of his bloodline. This blessing also determined what his son had a right to receive in the house.

The question is, What does our birthright entitle us to receive? And the answer is, Everything! The Bible says that God has blessed us with *"**all** spiritual blessings in Christ."* In other words, God has given us the full birthright in His Son Jesus. This birthright entitles us to certain privileges as born-again sons and daughters of the Most High God. We have been given full access to the blessings of God as citizens of His kingdom.

In another letter, the apostle Paul wrote, *"For our conversation is in heaven; from whence also we look for the Savior, the Lord Jesus Christ"* (Philippians 3:20). The word *"conversation"* is a very interesting term. It comes from the Greek word *politeuma*, which literally means "citizenship," or the constitution of a commonwealth and the laws by which it is administered. Several other Bible translations, including the *New American Standard Bible*, translate the term *"conversation"* as *"citizenship."* In other words, our citizenship, as well as its constitution, is in heaven. We have heavenly citizenship and a heavenly constitution. Whenever Satan attempts to oppress a born-again believer, he is literally violating his or her rights, as set forth in the heavenly constitution.

You Must Enforce Your Own Rights!

In the early 1960s, many southern states in America instituted a method of racial segregation known as "Jim Crow laws." These laws denied African-Americans and other minorities certain liberties that all American citizens should enjoy, according to the Constitution. During this time, African-Americans were prohibited from using public restrooms and from patronizing certain restaurants, movie theaters, and other venues. Many of them were beaten, mobbed, lynched, and even murdered, all in the name of Jim Crow. For many years, this policy was considered normal in the U.S., until certain brave individuals, such as the late Dr. Martin Luther King Jr., arose and challenged the system. He and others argued that the treatment of blacks in the south was "unconstitutional" and unjust.

Through the hard work, dedication, and sacrifice of these courageous individuals, the Civil Rights Act of 1964 was ultimately passed by the United States Congress. This act prohibited the mistreatment of any person based on the color of his skin. As a result of the bold stance of those individuals who refused to back down, segregation and Jim Crow laws were put to an end in America, and the United States became a nation known for its freedom, ethnic diversity, and multiculturalism.

How did this nation undergo such a drastic change? Simple! Someone placed a demand on the Constitution. In other words, someone insisted on being granted his or her constitutional rights! Beloved, we must do the same in our spiritual lives. Until we place a demand on God's Word and exercise the authority God has given us, nothing will change. The rights that you neglect to enforce will be the rights you will fail to enjoy. Before we can engage in effective spiritual warfare against the enemy, we must be well-informed as to what God's Word says about our covenant rights, and we must be willing to enforce those rights, in Jesus' name.

SATAN KNOWS THAT YOU HAVE AUTHORITY OVER HIM, BUT HE ATTEMPTS TO KEEP YOU IGNORANT OF THIS AUTHORITY.

The Right to Deliverance from Demonic Oppression

Some time ago, a woman came to one of our meetings in desperate need of prayer. She complained about severe back pain and other ailments that had been oppressing her for a long time. As she approached the altar for prayer, I noticed that something was not quite right with the situation. I couldn't help but sense a demonic presence surrounding her. This was no ordinary demonic presence; it was very strong. As she came closer, I felt this evil presence more and more. The Holy Spirit instructed me to ask her if she'd had any involvement in the occult, so I did, asking her specifically about Hinduism.

At first she hesitated, but then she reluctantly admitted to having been dedicated and marked as a young girl to Vishnu, one of the Hindu gods. All of a sudden, the demonic spirit began to manifest. This spirit caused her to shake violently and contorted her face and body. I commanded the demon to come out of her. To this, the demon responded audibly, "I do not want to leave. I have had her for a long time." I asked the young lady if she accepted Jesus as her Lord, and once she'd said yes, I told the spirits of witchcraft, false religion, and occultism that they had no more legal right to this woman and that they had to leave her body immediately.

As I made this declaration, she began coughing and vomiting; she was completely delivered shortly thereafter. As soon as the spirits of the occult had been cast out of her, the healing she had awaited for so long manifested instantly. This woman had been unaware of her right, as a believer in Jesus, to be delivered and healed. I knew what her rights were, and through the authority vested in me, I invoked those rights on her behalf. The moment I did this, the enemy had to flee.

Beloved, the same can be true for you, in every area of your life. What is it that has kept you bound by the devil? What is it that has you oppressed? What are you afraid of? What is defeating you? Whatever it is, you have a right to enjoy life, and life more abundantly.

The Right to Enjoy Life Abundant

Jesus said, "*The thief* [the devil; Satan] *cometh not, but for to steal, and to kill, and to destroy: I am come that they might have life, and that they might have it more abundantly*" (John 10:10). We must invoke the abundant life in order to experience it. This life is the *zoe* life of God—an existence marked by the Greek word for physical and spiritual life. In other words, this is the same quality of life that God has in Himself. This is the life that Jesus enjoyed during His earthly ministry, and this is the life that God has called you and me to enjoy on a daily basis.

The enemy does not want us to enjoy this abundant life. Instead, he wants to keep us slaves to fear, anxiety, depression, insomnia, lust, and other forms of oppression. He wants us to believe the lie that our situation will never get better. He desires to convince us that we will always be sick, broke, bound, and defeated. But the moment we become aware of our rights under the new covenant and begin to defend them is the moment we experience freedom and begin to walk in victory.

The Truth Will Set You Free

"Knowledge is power!" has become a common phrase. This simple yet profound statement has a parallel Scripture in the Bible: *"And ye shall know the truth, and the truth shall make you free"* (John 8:32). Unfortunately, this statement of Jesus is often taken outside of its proper biblical context.

Knowledge of the truth is essential if we are to experience the abundant life that God has ordained for all His children. The question is, What knowledge is the Bible referring to? For example, many people in the church are aware that there is such a thing as evil. Some are even well versed in specific Scriptures that seem to expose the enemy's schemes, and yet they still find themselves being oppressed by the devil. Why is this the case? It is actually quite simple: They don't *know* the truth! Sure, they may have head knowledge of the truth, but this is not the same as "knowing" in a biblical sense.

You must understand that there are two types of knowing. The first type, one with which most of us are familiar, is what I call "mental assent." Mental assent involves intellectually comprehending theological concepts and subsequently agreeing with them. An example of mental assent is Scripture memorization. Anyone with a basic intelligence level can memorize Bible verses. This is the introductory form of knowledge. However, this is not the knowledge Jesus was referring to in John 8:32.

The "knowledge" referenced in John's gospel is the second and most important type of knowledge, and that is *ginosko*—to "know," "be aware of," "feel," "perceive," "understand." This is a deeper level of knowledge than mere mental assent. Simply put, this is what is commonly called "revelation knowledge." This concept is taken from the Jewish idiom for physical intimacy, which comes across in Genesis 4:1: *"Adam **knew** Eve his wife; and she conceived...."* When we know (*ginosko*) something, it means that our knowledge is intimate, revelatory, and experiential. This kind of knowledge always produces something. Therefore, lasting change always begins with revelation.

Remember, it is not the truth that you hear but the truth that you know (*ginosko*) that will make you free. In the biblical sense, knowledge truly is power.

Rulers of the Darkness

Through Jesus, every believer has been given the right to live a life of freedom, wholeness, and tranquility. This doesn't mean that we will never face any challenges, only that it *is* possible for us to live a life devoid of internal chaos, turmoil, and bondage.

The apostle Paul gives the following description of the battle we're fighting:

> *For we wrestle not against flesh and blood, but against principalities, against powers, against the rulers of the darkness of this world, against spiritual wickedness in high places.*
>
> (Ephesians 6:12)

We will expound further on this passage of Scripture throughout the book. For now, I would like to place particular emphasis on the phrase "*rulers of the darkness of this world.*" What is the apostle Paul referring to? If you are a visual person, as I am, you might have a mental picture of Darth Vader of *Star Wars* or some other menacing villain from a science-fiction movie. Unfortunately, the darkness Paul refers to is much worse. Why? The word for "*rulers*" in this passage is the Greek word *kosmokratōr*, referring to the lord of the world, also called the prince of this age. What does this mean? It means that the ruler of the darkness of this age—Satan—has a measure of rule, or power, to lord over his domain.

And what is Satan's domain? He lords over "*the darkness of this world.*" The word "*darkness*" comes from the Greek word for "blindness" or "ignorance," which is *skotos*. In other words, Satan rules in the domain of ignorance and spiritual blindness. He desires to keep God's people oblivious to his activity in their lives and even more ignorant of the tools that God has made available to them in order to bring about his defeat.

The devil can operate effectively only in the darkness. This is why the first step to spiritual victory is knowing the truth. The fact is, there are many people who are battling things that they can't begin to identify or explain. Many believers in the church don't even realize they are under demonic oppression. They think it is simply an issue with their personality, a psychological battle, or an illness that runs in their family. They are completely unaware of the clandestine plot of the enemy to kill, steal, and destroy.

You may be able to identify with the aforementioned issues. You may be in the midst of a battle right now. You may have been struggling with a prolonged issue of sin, sickness, addiction, or defeat in your life, and you're frustrated that you have yet to see a breakthrough. My friend, if your struggle has been persistent and overpowering, it is likely that the "*ruler of the darkness of this* world" is behind it. He is the reason why so many Christians are suffering silently from depression, anxiety, fear, hopelessness, and other torments. The first step to defeating the enemy is learning the truth of God's Word. Once you realize what God says about you in His holy Word, you can easily identify—and eliminate—anything operating in your life that is contrary to the will of God.

A Lesson in Spiritual Warfare

Contrary to popular belief, spiritual warfare is not a ministry that some individuals are called to, nor is it just an activity we sign up to participate in at our local church. Spiritual warfare does not belong to a specific denomination or a select group of people. The truth is that each of us is already engaged in a spiritual battle. Spiritual warfare is not optional! There is a realm of darkness that we face on a daily basis. Whether you are aware of it or not, there is a battle being waged against you at every moment. The better you understand the nature of that battle, and the more thoroughly developed your weapons are, the better prepared you will be to fight and win.

For years, I was convinced that the problems I was facing in my life were just a part of the package, so to speak. I can remember one thought that repeatedly came to mind when I was a young boy: *Your parents aren't coming back!* From the first time I entertained that demonic thought, I would secretly anticipate something tragic happening to my family. I thought that, one day, I was going to receive "the call" telling me my parents had been killed in a horrible accident. At the time, I had no idea that this recurring thought was demonic. I just assumed it was a normal thought process.

The devil is a liar! (See John 8:44.) I finally realized that those thoughts were not my own but were rather the result of a spirit of fear waging war against my mind. Little did I know that the enemy would try to use similar strategies against me in the future.

THE ENEMY WAGES WAR AGAINST OUR MIND AND EMOTIONS TO BRING US INTO FEAR AND BONDAGE. GIVE HIM NO PLACE!

When my wife and I planted our first church, we encountered a level of spiritual warfare that was completely unexpected. Talk about on-the-job training! This spiritual battle nearly destroyed our ministry—and it almost ended my life, as I will explain in a later chapter. Since then, I have come to realize that Satan is not even remotely in the business of mercy, compassion, or empathy. He is absolutely ruthless. He is dead-set on destroying his victims without hesitation. He attempts to kill marriages, ministries, and moves of God before they even start.

This is why it's important that we learn to identify his strategies and neutralize his attacks. We do these things not through human reason, logic, or effort but through the power of the Holy Spirit. We must have revelation from the Word of God on how to walk in victory.

One day, I woke up and realized that the devil was occupying areas of my life that did not belong to him. So, I asked him politely to leave. Unfortunately, the devil is not a gentleman; kindness is not his forte. Soon, I realized that if I wanted him to go, I would have to evict him forcefully. And I believe that God is going to reveal to you the divine strategies that you need to know in order to evict the enemy from every area of your life, as well. You are going to take back your marriage and other relationships, your finances, your ministry, and your destiny. This is the essence of spiritual warfare. Once you understand the dynamics of spiritual warfare, you can effectively overcome every attack of the devil against your life. You will know the difference between a demonic attack and a problem that stems from your own flesh. You will discern what distinguishes your own thoughts from the satanic thoughts that the devil plants in your conscious mind and your subconscious life. These "spiritual skills" are crucial in winning spiritual battles.

Spiritual Warfare Defined

What do we mean by the term "spiritual warfare"? Most of us have probably heard this term used in a church setting, or maybe we've read about it in a Christian book. What does it really mean? The apostle Paul explains it well in the book of Ephesians, in the passage we've been considering:

> *For we wrestle not against flesh and blood, but against principalities, against powers, against the rulers of the darkness of this world, against spiritual wickedness in high places.*
> (Ephesians 6:12)

The term "*wrestle*" is an important part of spiritual warfare. It comes from the Greek word *pal*, which refers to a contest between two in which each endeavors to throw the other; the outcome is decided when the victor is able to hold his opponent down with his hand upon his neck. It serves as a word picture for the spiritual battle or struggle (literally "grapple") with the power of evil. Notice that this battle, or wrestling match, ends only when one person is standing over the other. Either you are going to conquer, or you are going to be conquered. When we speak of spiritual warfare, we are talking about our strategic engagement with—and ultimate victory over—the powers of darkness. (Again, by "powers of darkness," we mean Satan and his demons, which operate in the unseen realm.)

As I said before, spiritual warfare is not an optional activity. The moment you became born again, you were enlisted as a soldier in God's army. It is important to note that, from an ontological standpoint, the devil has already been defeated. Jesus disarmed the devil on the cross! The apostle Paul conveys this truth in Colossians 2:15: "*And having spoiled principalities and powers, he made a shew of them openly, triumphing over them in it.*"

Jesus has already triumphed over Satan. As a result, you and I are more than conquerors. (See Romans 8:37.) Why, then, do we have to engage in battle against the devil? As with any military conquest, there are always rogue factions that persist in their attempts to lay siege to territory that no longer belongs to them. In the same way, even though they know their defeat is sure, demonic spirits still seek to attack, enslave, torment, and oppress God's people. For this reason, their defeat must be enforced through strategic battles *waged by believers* that render them powerless.

The good news is that we are fighting a defeated foe. The more you recognize that the Lord Jesus has already defeated the enemy, the more spiritual authority you will exercise over the enemy, and the more confidence you will have as you come against the powers of darkness. This does not change the fact that there is still darkness in the earth; and, as long as this darkness exists, there will be spiritual antagonism. Later on, we will discuss the importance of knowing your spiritual identity as it relates to spiritual warfare. For now, I want to challenge you to shift your paradigm from a passive stance to an active posture.

Again, many Christians are demonized and don't even know it. As you move forward on this journey with me, you will learn how to recognize demonization, how to receive deliverance, and how to minister deliverance to others. Always remember where the battle rages: in the mind. When you achieve victory in the battlefield of your own mind, you will begin walking in lasting freedom and victory in every single area of your life.

Like spiritual warfare, deliverance is not a spiritual gift or a ministry reserved for a select few people in the church. Rather, every new covenant believer has the power, authority, and responsibility to walk in total deliverance and to minister deliverance to others.

Now I'd like to share the story of someone who took this responsibility seriously—and reaped great fruit as a result.

Gloria's Voice Restored

Gloria is a worship leader at our church. During the last week of the year 2013, she recognized that some of the promises the Lord had made to us concerning our lives and our ministry had not yet come to fruition. She was also feeling generally dissatisfied with her own spiritual life. So, she went on a weeklong "desperation journey" to seek the Lord. Recognizing that the Lord had been making an appeal to her to draw near to Him in the "secret place" and to "abide in the Vine," she read books about those topics, studied the precious Word of God, and prayed. She would wake at four in the morning, long before her kids were up, to seek the Lord in worship and prayer.

For a while, it felt like nothing was happening, yet something great was being birthed within her. At the next church service, on the last Sunday of 2013, she was preparing to lead worship when she felt that something was different. Her heart was different; the atmosphere was different—all because of her recent pursuit of the secret place. That Sunday, the evidence came: The worship was so gloriously filled with the presence of God that people were on the floor, wailing, during the service. Prophecy broke forth, and the glory of God engulfed the worshippers through her unrestrained worship.

THE ENEMY OFTEN ATTEMPTS TO SILENCE OUR VOICE IN ORDER TO REDUCE OUR EFFECTIVENESS AND INFLUENCE. INSTEAD OF BEING SILENCED, SILENCE THE ENEMY!

No one could get off the floor for what seemed like seconds but may well have been an hour. Two days later, at the New Year's Eve service, the glory of God fell once again; we looked at the clock and realized we had been in the glory for two hours, although it felt like only a minute had passed. It was almost midnight, so we rushed to complete the service.

Afterward, Gloria felt something trying to silence her voice. She described the feeling as being trapped inside a fish tank or a compression chamber, in which every sounded she made was muted. No matter how loud she would try to speak or sing, it seemed as if something was encapsulating her voice. She had a frightening dream in which her efforts to speak caused her entire mouth to twist into a knot incapable of producing any sound.

Within days, a tickle started in her throat, followed soon by a terrible cold. After that came the complete loss of her voice, accompanied by a sore throat, coughing, and hoarseness—the works. After the New Year's Eve service, she was unable to sing and could hardly talk. This was a demonic assault being made against her voice and against the power of God in her. The devil knew that if she had no voice, she wouldn't be able to prophesy or to minister healing and deliverance to anyone.

After ten weeks of frustration and forced silence, Gloria had had enough. She said, "Satan, no more. Get your hands off me!" Just before this happened, I had spoken with her and asked if she wanted to allow Satan to keep robbing her of her talents and afflicting her body. She said no, and went to war in the spirit.

One night, still frustrated by her inability to make much sound with her voice, Gloria was preparing to lead worship when the Lord said to her, "Forget about rehearsals; just focus on Me and worship Me." So, she put on some anointed worship music and quickly lost herself in the presence of God. About forty minutes into her worship, around midnight, the Lord said, "Now pray for your throat." She had already ascended into the presence of God, so she prayed confidently, without effort, "I declare that I am healed." While she prayed in faith, the Lord opened her eyes in the spirit to see what looked like two dark hands tightly wrapped around a cord. It was her vocal cords, being squeezed by the hands of a demonic entity. Once the Lord revealed this to her, she commanded those hands to be removed, and, in the spirit, she flicked off every finger, finally ripping off the hands. She declared her throat healed, and immediately she heard God say, "Now your throat is loosed." Instantly, her voice was restored.

The next morning, while Gloria was singing, she noticed her voice becoming hoarse again. So, she reminded the enemy, midway through a worship song, "Get your filthy hands off my throat—I am already healed." Her song flowed out like a glorious river, and a voice that had been demonically muted for months was restored by the glorious power of God.

Deliverance Prayer

I declare, by the name of Jesus, that I am strong and have already overcome the evil one, according to 1 John 2:14. I recognize in my spirit that the Lord Jesus Christ has already triumphed over the devil. Thank You, Lord, for winning the victory! I come against any demonic forces that would seek to confuse, attack, enslave, oppress, or otherwise torment me, and I declare them bound and cast out, in the mighty name of Jesus.

From this day forward, I make a conscious decision to embrace and walk in lasting freedom and victory. I embrace my kingdom assignment to engage the enemy in spiritual warfare, and I declare that I will not retreat or surrender to the wiles of the devil. I declare that every area of ignorance or foolishness is enlightened by the Word of God, and that I will never again walk in darkness, in Jesus' name! Amen.

WHO DO YOU THINK YOU ARE?

*And **ye are complete** in him, which is the head of all principality and power.*
—Colossians 2:10

One night many years ago, a friend of mine called and asked if he could come by my apartment to talk. We talked often, so there was nothing strange about his request; the thing that I found eerie, however, was the presence I felt while he spoke, even over the phone. At the time, another friend was visiting me, and I asked him to pray. In a matter of minutes, the friend who had called me arrived and knocked on my door. I let him inside, and we began talking. And then the unthinkable happened. His visage transformed right before my eyes. All of a sudden, a sinister grin appeared on his face, and a dark presence filled the room. He looked at me and said, "You think you are so special, don't you?" This didn't sound like the friend I knew! At this point, I began praying. "Who do you think you are?" he asked. At the time, I was not as familiar with deliverance or spiritual warfare as I am today, so the only thing I knew to say was, "I am a child of God!" I began taking authority over the spirits that were controlling my dear friend, and I commanded them to leave him, in Jesus' name. After I had done this, my friend—or, rather, the spirit operating within him—spoke and said, "I will rip you apart! I can really hurt you!"

This friend happened to be heavily involved in martial arts and was very capable of inflicting severe physical damage. The first thought that ran through my mind was, *Run!* Yet my body refused to move. All of a sudden, boldness rose up in my spirit as never before. I declared, "Satan, you can't hurt me! I am a child of the living God, and the blood of Jesus Christ covers me. In the name of the Lord Jesus, spirit of death, murder, and wickedness, come out of him now!" Instantly, he began snarling like an animal, and then he fell to the floor under the power of God. The ground literally shook beneath my feet. Within minutes, he returned to his normal self. Hallelujah to the Lamb!

This was one of my first encounters with demonization and subsequent deliverance. This was also one of the first times I realized the importance of knowing our identity when we engage in spiritual warfare. In fact, knowing our identity in Christ is the secret to releasing the spiritual authority that we need to conquer to enemy.

YOUR KINGDOM IDENTITY IS A KEY COMPONENT TO EXERCISING SPIRITUAL AUTHORITY.

Since the episode I just described, I have had several encounters with the demonic, and I have seen countless people set free from the grip of darkness. Each of these experiences has confirmed that one of the most important aspects of successful spiritual warfare is knowing our identity in Christ. By "identity," I mean the unique attributes that make us who we are as believers. Our identity is our essential character that constitutes our authentic selves. Before we can experience lasting freedom from demonic oppression, or liberate others from it, we must know who we are—and *whose* we are. In fact, the devil's worst nightmare is that the body of Christ, His bride, will learn who she really is.

Every promise and blessing in the Word of God hinges on the issue of identity. If you want to walk in victory over the enemy, you must learn what God says about who you really are. The moment I learned who I was in Christ was the moment the tyrannical grip of bondage was broken off my life. Beloved, you have a kingdom identity that is far greater than even the best part of your natural identity. You have a supernatural DNA!

Identity: The Carrier of Authority

Colossians 2:10 says that we, as believers in God, are complete in Him who is the head of all principality and power. What does this statement mean? The word *"complete"* in this verse comes from the Greek word *plēroō*, which means to make full, to fill, to cause to abound, to supply liberally, and to fill to the brim. This expression is used frequently throughout the Bible, especially in reference to the Holy Spirit. For example, Ephesians 5:18 commands us to *"be filled with the Spirit."* However, the implication of *"complete,"* in this verse from Colossians, is "to be brought to a state of fullness or fulfillment."

This is a statement about our identity. You and I have been made whole, complete, and overflowing in Christ. In Him, there is nothing missing and nothing broken. Our fullness is in Jesus Christ. Do you really believe that? The explosive power of this statement is revealed in its magnitude in the statement that follows, describing Christ: "[He] *is the head of* **all** *principality and* *power."* This is absolutely amazing! We are complete in Christ, and Christ is the head of all principality and power, which means that we have the ability to exercise headship and authority over any and every principality that exists in the spiritual realm—so long as we are walking in the consciousness of our true spiritual identity.

This authority is inherent in our very nature; it is part and parcel of our spiritual identity. How is that for a Sunday school lesson? The word for *"head"* in Colossians 2:10 is the Greek word *kephalē*, which means chief, supreme, or prominent. Just as the entire body receives directives from the brain and cannot survive without the head, so you and I are inextricably connected to the Lord Jesus Christ. Our brain delivers commands to our various body parts through the central nervous system. Any activity in our body affects the brain, and vice versa. When was the last time you saw a foot isolate itself and totally disregard the brain's instructions to walk? This would be considered a neurological disorder, because the extremity is operating autonomously from the brain and nervous system.

Our life and identity are derived from the "head" to which we are connected. This spiritual identity is, in essence, the carrier or container of our divine authority. The reason why we have authority is because we are in Christ. He is our head! His authority is on the inside of us. We cannot function, let alone operate in authority, independently of Him.

THE AGENDA OF THE DEVIL AND HIS DEMONS IS TO INTERRUPT BELIEVERS' CONSCIOUSNESS OF JESUS AND MANIPULATE THEM INTO OPERATING INDEPENDENTLY OF HIM.

Too many believers are not walking in their kingdom identity because they refuse to acknowledge their head—the Lord Jesus.

Consequently, they are not aware of who they are or whose they are. As a result, they are unable to weather the storms of spiritual attacks that come against them. Like the foot mentioned earlier, many believers are attempting to have an identity outside of Christ. Beloved, that is simply not possible! We are complete in Him alone; any other identity is a false identity. Furthermore, our identity is what carries our authority. Without our connection to Jesus, we would be completely helpless against the enemy.

A spiritual identity crisis is the root cause of insecurity and anxiety about oneself, and insecurity is the force behind all fear—an emotion that energizes the realm of darkness. You cannot exercise authority over that which you fear. If you are insecure about who you are and whose you are, the devil will use fear to manipulate and control you. Beloved, give him no place!

Who's Your Daddy?

For ye have not received the spirit of bondage again to fear; but ye have received the Spirit of adoption, whereby we cry, **Abba, Father.** (Romans 8:15)

I cannot emphasize enough the importance of knowing who we are and, even more important, *whose* we are. When we know to whom we belong, we can walk in security and confidence.

What does this have to do with spiritual warfare, you ask? Every spiritual battle that we face is essentially a battle for identity. The more confident we are in our true spiritual identity, the more victorious we will be in spiritual battle. The devil tries to convince God's people that their heavenly Father doesn't love them—that He is a harsh judge who does not pardon them or set them free. And when he manages to distort our perception of God, he gains access to our heart, soul, and mind.

I often think of the devil as a spiritual human trafficker. The first thing that a human trafficker does when he abducts a young woman is to convince her that her natural father doesn't love her. He tells her that he is her real father now. The goal is to create a psychological dependence on the oppressor. Eventually, the woman will see the pimp or human trafficker as her daddy, the one who affirms her and gives her value. The psychological phenomenon in which hostages express empathy for, and experience positive feelings toward, their captors, sometimes to the point of identifying with them, is called Stockholm syndrome, or capture-bonding.

Beloved, it's tragic but true—many believers are suffering from a spiritual Stockholm syndrome. They have come to embrace the spiritual oppression in their lives as normal or acceptable. Many are even defensive when presented with the notion of freedom. There is only one way to break free from this kind of spiritual oppression, and it is through the power of God's unconditional, irrepressible love.

WHEN WE KNOW THAT WE ARE LOVED AND ACCEPTED BY OUR HEAVENLY FATHER, WE CAN BREAK FREE FROM THE SHACKLES OF FEAR AND INSECURITY.

Romans 8:15 is one of the most powerful verses in the Bible. It's so important that I'll state it again: *"For ye have not received the spirit of bondage again to fear; but ye have received the Spirit of adoption, whereby we cry,* **Abba, Father.***"* The word "bondage" comes from the Greek word *douleia*, which means "slavery." God has not given us a spirit of fear, which enslaves; instead, He has given us the Spirit of adoption, which is another name for the Holy Spirit. The Spirit of adoption affirms, validates, and empowers us, so that we need not fear. The fear indicated in Romans 8:15 is dread, or terror. It is the fear that an orphan feels inside his soul—the fear of being alone, abandoned, without an identity.

In other words, through Jesus Christ and the Holy Spirit, we have received spiritual "sonship," which enables us to identify God as *"Abba,"* or *"Daddy"*—a term of intimacy and endearment. God is our daddy, and we can call upon Him without any sense of shame or guilt. When this revelation soaks into your soul, it will change your life forever. And it is a key to winning the battle against the enemy!

Overcoming the Orphan Spirit

And the evil spirit answered and said, Jesus I know, and Paul I know; but who are ye? (Acts 19:15)

Earlier, we mentioned that it is impossible to exercise authority over something you fear. It is equally impossible to carry the authority of someone you don't know. Remember, there is an inextricable connection between identity and authority. In the book of Acts, chapter 19, we are given an account of some vagabond Jews who were exorcists, attempting to cast out demons in the name of Jesus *"whom Paul preacheth"* (Acts 19:13). Notice that the Bible refers to them as vagabonds. (See verse 13.) This was a physical reality as well as a spiritual one. What does the term "vagabond" mean? A vagabond is a person who wanders from place to place without a home. These vagabond Jews were attempting to mimic what they had seen Paul doing. In other words, they were attempting to exercise spiritual authority without having a relationship with the Source of that authority. To this, the demon responded, *"Jesus I know, and Paul I know; but who are ye?"*

THE SPIRITUAL ENTITIES OF THE REALM OF DARKNESS ARE WELL AWARE OF WHETHER WE HAVE A RELATIONSHIP WITH GOD.

What happened next is almost shocking:

And the man in whom the evil spirit was leaped on them, and overcame them, and prevailed against them, so that they fled out of that house naked and wounded. (Acts 19:16)

The demon did not yield to the authority of those vagabond Jews because their authority was not legitimate. As a result, they were tormented by the same demons they had been attempting to cast out.

The vagabond Jews in this passage were operating out of what is called an "orphan spirit"—a spirit of insecurity birthed from a lack of intimacy and connection to God as Father. It is this orphan spirit that gives birth to "spiritual vagabonds," nominal believers who are incapable of walking in real authority because they lack the requisite intimacy with God that imparts true authority.

Beloved, there are many people today who are operating as spiritual orphans and spiritual vagabonds. Remember, spiritual power and authority are the direct result of knowing our identity in Christ. The exorcists in Acts 19 were trying to imitate Paul's power without possessing his foundation of intimacy with God. They were spiritual imposters! And there continue to be many spiritual imposters in the body of Christ today. This is one reason why many people have been praying for years, to no avail, that certain strongholds would be broken. The problem is that they don't know who they are! They are not convinced that the Father loves them unconditionally. As a result, they are trying to execute formulas instead of manifesting genuine authority that stems from a deep relationship with their heavenly Father.

If we are going to dominate the demonic realm, we must establish and understand our identity as sons and daughters of the King of Kings. We must allow the power of God's love to break the orphan spirit and uproot it from within us.

Listen to the Holy Spirit, Who Testifies to Your Identity

Are you a child of God? If so, then the Holy Spirit will provide a confirmation deep within. The apostle Paul testifies to this fact in the book of Romans, where he writes, *"The Spirit itself beareth witness with our spirit, that we are the children of God"* (Romans 8:16). In other words, the Holy Spirit bears joint witness with our human spirit that we are no longer "bastards," illegitimate children, but indeed sons and daughters of God.

Again, the identity that the Holy Spirit affirms is the root of our genuine spiritual authority. We are no longer orphans or vagabonds, because God has adopted us into His royal family and granted us all the rights and privileges of natural children. The Greek word for *"children"* used in the above verse from Romans is the word *teknon*, which means "dear children" or "the children of His love." We are not only made sons and daughters in Christ; we are also given the precious title of "dear children."

Overcome Any Spiritual Identity Crises

The devil knows that our spiritual identity is key in defeating him; therefore, he continually attempts to throw the church into a spiritual identity crisis. Through deception, the enemy tries to convince you that you are not a child of God but rather an illegitimate son or daughter. How does he attempt to do this? He uses sin, addiction, infirmities, guilt, shame, rejection, and other forms of torment to convince you that your identity is that which has you bound. If you see yourself only in light of your sins and failures, then you will never be able to embrace the supernatural power that God has made available for you that will ultimately set you free.

This is why the enemy incites the people of God to rebel against Him—as long as they are walking contrary to God's will for their lives, they will inevitably be filled with chaos and confusion. I regularly talk with and minister to people who are in a perpetual state of spiritual chaos and calamity. In their mind, they have become their most egregious sin or habit. Instead of recognizing that they are more than conquerors through Him who loves them, they have embraced the lies of the enemy. This is not God's will!

UNLESS WE CONFESS AND CAST OFF SIN, DISOBEDIENCE, AND REBELLION, THEY WILL CAUSE US TO FALL VICTIM TO SPIRITUAL CONFUSION AND BONDAGE.

You are not your addiction. You are not your sinful behavior. You are not whatever has you bound. You are a child of God. And until you truly know your identity, you will never be able to break free from the devil. In fact, at the root of any and all addictions is an identity crisis.

The ministry of the Holy Spirit is to testify of our identity as children of God and to bring us to a place of true, lasting freedom from the devil and his wiles. He accomplishes this task by revealing to us, and reminding us of, who we are in Christ. Instead of identifying with the thing you are struggling with, declare out loud, "I am a child of the living God! I am an overcomer, because greater is He who lives in me than he who is in the world. I am not what I used to be, for God has made me a new creation in Christ Jesus!"

Deliverance Prayer

Father, in the name of Jesus Christ, I thank You for who You are and for all that You have done for me. I declare that any and all traces of the orphan spirit working in my life or mind, whether consciously or subconsciously, are removed, in Jesus' name. As an act of my faith and free will, I embrace the unconditional love of the Father and declare that I am accepted into the beloved family of God. I take authority over any and all spirits of rejection, insecurity, inferiority, despondency, and self-hatred, in Jesus' name.

From today onward, I choose to walk in the Father's love in every area of my life. I take authority over any demonic spirits, sins, and/or addictions that have entered my soul through the gateway of rejection, right now! I possess the mind of Christ; therefore, I reject any thoughts or suggestions of insecurity or inferiority, in the mighty name of Jesus. My Father loves me, and through His love, I am empowered to overcome every assault of the evil one on my mind and emotions, in Jesus' name. Amen!

4

BEDTIME STORIES

*Thou shalt not be afraid for the terror by night;
nor for the arrow that flieth by day.*
—Psalm 91:5

Late one summer night, when I was seventeen, I suddenly became aware of a presence in my bedroom. This was not an ordinary presence but something dark and malevolent. It seemed that there was something or someone hovering over my bed. A sense of fear overwhelmed my entire body as I felt what seemed like hands prying my mouth open and then a knife piercing my skull. I was completely paralyzed, unable to even speak, as this dark force kept its grip on my body. I felt like I was having a seizure. After several minutes, there was a release, and the darkness lifted. I was so afraid that I ran from my bedroom into my father's room. The only feeling I can remember was one of absolute terror. The thought of going back to sleep was horrific. I prayed to the Lord and asked Him to protect me from this evil and to never allow that dark presence to assault me again.

I wish that I could say that was the last time I had an experience of this nature. Unfortunately, it was not. The event that I just described was not an alien abduction, an extraterrestrial visit, or an epileptic seizure. It was a demonic attack, though I didn't realize it at the time. And I am just one of many people who have experienced this terrifying type of encounter. I have ministered to thousands of people within the body of Christ who have been gripped by a menacing force in the night or tormented by nightmares. For many, this demonic activity has manifested in the form of anxiety attacks, chronic fear, or a specific phobia; for countless others, demonic forces have attacked their minds, their emotions, and even their physical bodies.

Whether you can directly relate to my experience is completely irrelevant. What is relevant, however, is the fact that there is a realm of darkness operating inconspicuously behind the curtains of your life, the sole agenda of which is to bring you into bondage.

THE SOONER YOU LEARN TO RECOGNIZE THE ENEMY'S TACTICS, THE SOONER YOU CAN DISPEL THE DARKNESS FROM YOUR LIFE.

After this terrifying episode, I went to the only person I knew would understand: my pastor. He explained to me that what I had experienced that night was actually demonic oppression. It was the first time I had ever heard the term. He told me to plead the blood of Jesus and to apply anointing oil in and around my bedroom. I gladly obliged, and the demonic attacks eventually ceased, to my great relief. It's terrible to think how long these assaults might have gone on if I hadn't consulted my pastor and discovered just what I was dealing with.

Perhaps this is the first time you are hearing about demonic oppression. "Oppression" is defined as "prolonged cruel or unjust treatment or control." Thus, demonic oppression is the persecution, abuse, and tyranny afflicted on God's people by the evil one.

We know, based on the authority of Scripture, that born-again believers in Jesus cannot be possessed (owned) by the devil; however, it is clearly possible for believers to be oppressed.

Earlier, we discussed Satan's position as the prince of this age and the ruler of the darkness (i.e., ignorance and spiritual blindness) of this world. This means that Satan has a legal jurisdiction in which he is still permitted to operate. And fear is the primary *modus operandi* by which he operates and wields his influence.

Who's Living in Your House?

I want to share with you a story that I heard several years ago. Two young brothers were playing around in their bedroom one day when they made a bone-chilling discovery. One of the brothers accidentally bumped against a built-in bookcase that opened, revealing a secret passageway connecting to a spiral staircase. Taking along a flashlight, the brothers went down the stairs to investigate and found a secret room, with plenty of indications that someone had been living there, including food, silverware, and toys. Someone had actually been staying in this family's home without their knowledge. They were shocked when they found out that the original homeowners had incorporated a series of secret passageways into the infrastructure when it was built. This mystery tenant had been coming and going clandestinely for several years—quite possibly for a longer period of time than this family had lived in the home.

I wish that I could say that this was a scene from a horror movie, but it was not. Some have posited that the story was a hoax.* Regardless, it goes to show that you don't always know what's living in your house—or what's lurking in your life.

---

* See Liz Klimas, "Hoax? Kids Find a Secret Room Hidden Behind a Bookcase in Their House — and That Was Only the Beginning," *The Blaze* (November 14, 2013), http://www.theblaze.com/stories/2013/11/14/the-moment-when-kids-find-a-secret-room-behind-a-bookcase-find-out-what-was-inside/.

Evicting Demonic Spirits

Many people in the body of Christ are unknowingly harboring demonic forces in their lives. These spiritual "unwanted guests" are exploiting "secret passageways" in many believers' minds, emotions, and belief systems. They are undermining marriages, stealing peace, and devouring the health of millions in the body of Christ. You can't evict a tenant of whom you are unaware! I believe that this is the reason why so many people are being tormented, afflicted, oppressed, and abused by demonic spirits. These spirits enter in, secretly and sporadically, to torment their victims without their knowledge. They conceal themselves in the hidden compartments of a believer's life and often perpetuate this oppression for years on end.

REVELATION KNOWLEDGE IS THE KEY TO OVERCOMING DEMONIC OPPRESSION AND CLOSING THE DOOR TO DEMONIC ACTIVITY.

Demonic oppression can take many forms: addiction, depression, anger, bitterness, suicidal thoughts, and so forth. Any pervasive thought pattern, behavior, mind-set, illness, or emotional state that brings you under ungodly control and/or keeps you from fulfilling the plan and purpose of God for your life is a form of demonic oppression.

This all sounds scary, but we can't afford to be afraid! We have this charge in Psalm 91:5: *"Thou shall not be afraid for the terror by night...."* This is a command from God. We are commanded to not be afraid of terror—even the kind that strikes by night. The word for *"terror"* in this verse comes from the Hebrew word *pachad*, which means "dread." This refers to something that we anticipate with great apprehension.

It is not the will of God for you to live in fear or apprehension. When I first experienced demonic oppression, I didn't realize that the devil was literally infringing upon my God-ordained rights. Beloved, you and I cannot afford to be in fear, because fear produces torment. (See 1 John 4:18.) Fear also undermines our confidence in our identity and our covenantal rights as children of God.

The turnaround in my life came only after I had a revelation of the authority I possessed in Christ and also came to understand how to use the name of Jesus to defeat the enemy.

Evicting the Spirits of Incubus and Succubus

On a mission trip to Africa, I noticed a very strange phenomenon. As I was praying for the young women in one of our crusades, many of them began to contort and manifest demonically. Some of these women even bowed over in a frozen, lifeless state for minutes at a time. Eventually, these women were set free by the power of God, but I couldn't help wondering why this demonic oppression was affecting such a large number.

After our meetings, I consulted with the host pastors concerning these strange manifestations, and they identified the culprits as "marine spirits." Apparently, there is a belief in West Africa that disembodied evil spirits attempt to attach themselves to women through sexual immorality. According to the pastors, many of the young women in the region had reported having experienced sexual encounters in their sleep. Women who were pregnant often reported experiencing miscarriages as a result. Though this spirit was referred to as a "marine spirit," I realized that it was the manifestation of a team of demonic spirits commonly referred to as Incubus and Succubus.

In ancient tradition, Incubus was a demonic spirit that would have sexual relations with women in their sleep, while Succubus was the spirit that would do the same thing with men. These demonic encounters were said to cause barrenness, sickness, and even death. Unfortunately, this spirit is not only present and active in the Third World. I have spoken with many people in the United States and abroad who have had these types of demonic encounters in their sleep. For example, many people have reported that they have experienced lustful or sexual dreams—often involving pornography—after which they awoke feeling defiled and unclean. Others have said that they felt as if they were being sexually assaulted while they were sleeping.

Beloved, these occurrences are not normal. I believe that these are manifestations of the demonic spirits referred to as Incubus and Succubus.

> **YOU MUST RECOGNIZE THAT THERE IS NO SPIRIT GREATER THAN THE NAME OF JESUS. WHEN YOU USE THE NAME OF JESUS, EVERY DEMON MUST FLEE.**

Some of you reading this book may have had an experience similar to those mentioned above but have not known what to do about it. You probably didn't even know what to call it! Very few people have the spiritual understanding to deal with such things. However, I want to remind you that you no longer need to be afraid. No longer must you be tormented in your sleep by unclean spirits or be oppressed in your mind by sexual perversion—you can be free! Whether you are dealing with an Incubus or Succubus spirit or some other form of demonic oppression, your response should be the same: You must decide today that you are no longer going to be bound and tormented by the enemy. We have seen countless people set free from the grip of sexual uncleanness.

The Bible admonishes us to *"flee fornication"* (1 Corinthians 6:18). The word *"fornication"* comes from the Greek word *porneia*, which refers to illicit sexual intercourse or sexual immorality. This includes any sexually perverse act committed against the body. Satan's agenda is to keep you bound up in guilt and shame so that you cannot serve the Lord, but you must give him no place! Today, I declare that all spirits of uncleanness are broken off your life, in Jesus' mighty name. Amen!

Drive the Devil Away

When I discuss spiritual warfare, I often refer to a story from the Old Testament about one of the great patriarchs of our faith, Abraham. The Bible records a divine encounter Abraham had with God that, I believe, offers us several profound insights into spiritual warfare. Let's read the biblical account, and then I'll paraphrase it before explaining its symbolic significance.

> *And* [the Lord] *said unto* [Abraham, then called Abram], *I am the* Lord *that brought thee out of Ur of the Chaldees, to give thee this land to inherit it. And he said, Lord* God, *whereby shall I know that I shall inherit it? And he said unto him, Take me an heifer of three years old, and a she goat of three years old, and a ram of three years old, and a turtledove, and a young pgeon. And he took unto him all these, and divided them in the midst, and laid each piece one against another: but the birds divided he not. And when the fowls came down upon the carcases, Abram drove them away.*
>
> (Genesis 15:7–11)

God made a covenant with Abraham in which He promised to make him the father of many nations, even though both he and his wife were well beyond their childbearing years. This promise also included an inheritance of land. To confirm the promise, God commanded Abraham to build and altar and to sacrifice a heifer, a female goat, a ram, a turtledove, and a young pigeon.

In ancient Semitic culture, covenants were made through the shedding of blood, using animals to symbolize the blood of the two parties entering into the covenant. It was customary for the two parties to cut the animals into pieces and to walk between the divided bodies, thereby sealing the covenant they were making.

Covenants among men were common enough in Abraham's day, but a covenant with the Creator of the universe? This was an epic moment indeed! By this covenant, Abraham and his entire bloodline would receive a supernatural transfer of unprecedented blessings.

There was one thing that Abraham did not anticipate as he prepared to cut the covenant with God, however, and that was *"the fowls."* After he had gone through all the necessary preparations for the sacrifice, a flock of predatory birds descended, ready to devour the animals he was about to burn as a pleasing aroma to God.

Beloved, there is more to this passage of Scripture than meets the eye. It serves as a prophetic picture of spiritual warfare. The fowls that descended to devour the sacrifice represent the demonic spirits that seek to block God's blessings from our lives. The enemy was trying to hinder Abraham from receiving the prophetic promises that God had ordained for him and his descendants. And he tries to do the same in your life!

Abraham had enough faith to determine that he wouldn't allow these fowls to steal what rightfully belonged to him, and so he *"drove them away."* The verb used to describe this action comes from the Hebrew word *nashab*, which means "to disperse," or to "(cause to) blow [away]."

We must adopt the same determination that Abraham had and drive away the forces of darkness from our lives. Don't just sit there and allow the enemy to molest you or steal from you; drive him away, in Jesus' name! Refuse to give the devil access to your prophetic promises. Just as Abraham did, we must open our mouths and proclaim God's Word. When we do, the Holy Spirit, who is the wind of God, will literally "blow away" the demonic oppression operating in our lives. You have the authority—now it's time to use it!

To prepare ourselves to drive away the enemy, we first need to familiarize ourselves with some of his key strategies so that we'll be able to outwit him.

The Four Strategies of the Enemy

The Bible warns us, *"Be sober, be vigilant; because your adversary the devil, as a roaring lion, walketh about, seeking whom he may devour"* (1 Peter 5:8). Notice that the devil *seeks* whom he may devour. Why is this important to highlight? He cannot devour everyone. Just as a natural lion cannot devour an entire herd of buffalo, neither can the devil successfully devour every believer. He preys on those who are vulnerable—those who don't understand their identity in Christ or the authority they possess as His children.

The word *"devour"* comes from the Greek word *katapinō*, which means to "drink down," or destroy. Remember, Jesus said in John 10:10, *"The thief cometh not, but for to steal, and to kill, and to destroy...."*

It is quite fascinating that the Bible associates the devil with a lion, because lions are commonly known as alpha predators. An alpha predator (also called an apex predator) is at the very top of the food chain because it has no natural predators, and it maintains its ecosystem by devouring more vulnerable animals. Apex predators thrive off of such tactics as fear, manipulation, and control. For example, lions usually do not hunt during the day but wait until nightfall to stalk their prey. Like the lion, the devil takes advantage of "reduced visibility" to catch his victims unawares. And just as a lion kills its prey through means of strangulation and suffocation, the enemy of your soul attempts to get a stranglehold on your mind, will, and emotions, in a vicious attempt to "suffocate" you through alienation from the abundant life in Christ.

THE DEVIL CONCEALS HIMSELF IN DARKNESS AND EXPLOITS EVERY OPPORTUNITY TO POUNCE ON BELIEVERS AND BRING DESTRUCTION INTO THEIR LIVES.

There are four different means through which the enemy attacks the believer and attempts to fill his life with discouragement, defeat, despair, and, ultimately, death. Once you understand these methods, or strategies, you will be better equipped to identify, subvert, and neutralize every demonic assault that Satan launches against you.

The four strategies of Satan are (1) temptation, (2) deception, (3) distraction, and (4) oppression. The devil has no creativity. Every attack in a believer's life will fall into one of these four categories. We will explore them now, beginning with temptation.

1. Temptation

Watch and pray, that ye enter not into temptation: the spirit indeed is willing, but the flesh is weak.   (Matthew 26:41)

The first and most common strategy that the enemy uses against believers is temptation. While there are several nuances in this term, as it's used in the Bible, the one that is mentioned most frequently in the New Testament goes by the Greek word *peirasmos*, which refers to an enticement to sin arising from desire or outward circumstances.

There are many areas in which we are tempted; however, the Bible says that the object of our temptation will always fall within three categories: *"the lust of the flesh,...the lust of the eyes,* [or] *the pride of life"* (1 John 2:16). The *"lust of the flesh"* encompasses any desires that arise from the sensuous nature of man. In other words, the lust of the flesh is man's proclivity toward the five senses: touch, taste, smell, sight, and hearing.

When we are born again, God gives us a brand-new nature, which is continually renewed in the image of our Creator and heavenly Father. (See Colossians 3:10.) However, there is still the issue of the flesh (*sarx*, in Greek). Again, when we speak of the "flesh," we are referring to the unregenerate part of our mind and body that seeks to alienate us from the new life residing in our spirit. An example of a temptation of the flesh would be the immoral thoughts that entice the mind, such as lust, uncleanness, and perversion.

The *"lust of the eyes"* refers to the desires that arise in us by virtue of what we see. Job said, *"I made a covenant with mine eyes; why then should I think upon a maid?"* (Job 31:1). In other words, Job understood that what he gazed upon had a direct effect on the desires of his heart. Along these same lines, Jesus said, *"Whosoever looketh on a woman to lust after her hath committed adultery with her already in his heart"* (Matthew 5:28). In other words, indulging in sinful thoughts that stem from what you see is tantamount to acting on those sinful thoughts.

What are you looking at? Does in honor the Lord? Whatever you look upon is what you will gravitate toward.

The third area of temptation identified by the Bible, the *"pride of life"* refers to presumption, self-will, and self-reliance—an attitude that trusts in earthly things and in one's own self rather than in God. Simply put, the pride of life is vanity.

Again, temptation is Satan's go-to tactic when attempting to attack believers. But, praise God, we need not fall for this scheme. We have the following reassurance in Paul's first epistle to the church at Corinth:

> *There hath no temptation taken you but such as is common to man: but God is faithful, who will not suffer you to be tempted above that ye are able; but will with the temptation also make a way to escape, that ye may be able to bear it.*
>
> (1 Corinthians 10:13)

GOD IS NOT THE AUTHOR OF TEMPTATION; TEMPTATION OCCURS WHEN WE ARE DRAWN AWAY BY OUR OWN DESIRES AND ENTICED.

We see from the above Scripture that temptation is common to mankind, and that God has given us a way of escape, so that we might overcome every temptation we face. The more conscious you are that God has already given you a way of escape, the more easily you will be able to overcome temptation.

Jesus modeled this during His earthly ministry, during which even He was not exempt from the devil's temptations. The fourth chapter of the gospels of Matthew and Luke relate Jesus' temptation by the devil in the wilderness—a period of forty days during which He fasted from food. Many scholars believe that He nearly reached the point of starvation. Along came the enemy, and he said, *"If thou be the Son of God, command that these stones be made bread"* (Matthew 4:3; see also Luke 4:3). I'm sure it was very tempting. But Jesus offered this response: *"It is written, Man shall not live by bread alone, but by every word that proceedeth out of the mouth of God"* (Matthew 4:4; see also Luke 4:4). Jesus overcame temptation by declaring God's Word—not once but three times. (See also Matthew 4:5–11; Luke 4:5–13.)

Beloved, we have at our disposal this very means of overcoming temptation. God's Word is the "way of escape" promised in 1 Corinthians 10:13! When we testify to the Word of God and of our belief in Jesus, the incarnate Word (see, for example, John 1:1), we put the enemy in his place.

In the book of Revelation, John describes how the believers "*overcame him* [Satan] *by the blood of the Lamb, and by the word of their testimony*" (Revelation 12:11). We will overcome Satan and his schemes—fear, lust, pride, hurt, disappointment, demonic attacks, and every type of temptation—by the blood of Jesus and by the Word of God!

Jesus overcame every temptation because He was completely sold out to the Word of God. Yielding to temptation will hinder the blessings and breakthrough that you desire from God, so you must refuse to yield to the enemy's schemes. Stand on the Word of God, say no to temptation, and defeat the devil!

2. Deception

And Adam was not deceived, but the woman being deceived was in the transgression. (1 Timothy 2:14)

Another tactic the enemy uses to ensnare God's people is deception—acts of mystification and subterfuge designed to beguile or propagate beliefs that are not true. In short, it is a strategy used to trick a person into believing a lie and to further seduce him into acting on that lie. The Bible records that Eve was deceived, or beguiled, by the serpent in the garden of Eden. The Bible also tells us that Satan (the serpent) was subtler than any other creature in the garden:

Now the serpent was more subtil than any beast of the field which the LORD *God had made. And he said unto the*

> *woman, Yea, hath God said, Ye shall not eat of every tree of the garden?* (Genesis 3:1)

Satan's nature is inherently deceptive. Notice that the devil's deception began with a question—one meant to cast doubt on the authenticity and truth of God's Word: *"Yea, hath God said, Ye shall not eat of every tree of the garden?"* This was a suggestive question meant to instigate obstinacy and rebellion in Eve, and it's exactly what the enemy of our soul uses against the children of God today. "Did God really mean it when He said that He would never leave you or forsake you?" "You're just human, aren't you?" "Do you really think you will ever get free?" These questions, in the form of thoughts and subtle suggestions, are nothing more than deceptive tactics by the evil one. You can rest assured that if it came out of the devil's mouth, it is an absolute lie. Why? Because Jesus tells us that the devil is incapable of telling the truth:

> [The devil]...*was a murderer from the beginning, and abode not in the truth, because there is no truth in him. When he speaketh a lie, he speaketh of his own: for he is a liar, and the father of it.* (John 8:44)

THE ONLY WAY SATAN CAN GAIN ACCESS TO YOUR LIFE IS THROUGH DECEPTION. EVERY AREA OF BONDAGE IN A BELIEVER'S LIFE CAN BE TRACED TO A LIE HE OR SHE HAS BELIEVED.

The Bible says that there is no truth in the wicked one. In fact, he is referred to as the "father of lies." The word *"liar"* in John 8:44 comes from the Greek word *pseustēs*, which refers to one who breaks faith. Satan's sole agenda is to "break your faith." That's what he did to Eve. By causing her to question God's instructions, he weakened her faith in God and enticed her to believe a lie. What was the lie? The lie was that she and Adam were incomplete. The lie was this: "If you eat of the fruit, *'ye shall not surely die: for God doth know that in the day ye eat thereof, then your eyes shall be opened, and ye shall be gods, knowing good and evil'*" (Genesis 3:4–5). What a gross falsehood!

Adam and Eve were already children of God, endowed with His supernatural power and authority. There was nothing missing and nothing broken—until they ate the fruit from the tree. The moment they ate of this forbidden fruit, the human race was forever altered. Fear, guilt, and shame were ushered in for the first time, and the first human beings came under the bondage of the wicked one.

Even though Satan still works his deceptions in the lives of believers today, we need not be ignorant of his schemes. When we know God and His Word, as we emphasized in our discussion of temptation, then we won't be prone to question Him; we won't be easily deceived by the evil one.

3. Distraction

> *Lest Satan should get an advantage of us: for we are not ignorant of his devices.* (2 Corinthians 2:11)

If the enemy is unsuccessful at getting a believer to yield to temptation or to fall prey to deception, his next strategy is distraction. Distraction is anything that prevents a person from giving full attention to what he ought to be focused on. In using this scheme, the enemy attempts to divert our thoughts, our emotional energies, and even our worship, away from God. You may not realize it, but many of the struggles you deal with in life are nothing more than mere distractions designed to absorb your spiritual energy. Many people are so focused on their personal problems—sickness, depression, lack, and so forth—that they hardly see God in their circumstances. They may not see Him at all.

Paul understood this concept all too well. In his epistle to the Romans, he wrote, *"Now I beseech you, brethren, mark them which cause divisions and offences contrary to the doctrine which ye have learned; and avoid them"* (Romans 16:17).

The word *"offences"* in this passage comes from the Greek word *skandalon,* which means "a trap-stick" or a "snare." The same term is used to refer to a trap set by a hunter. When hunting fowl or another type of animal, people often use bait to lure the animal into a trap; once the animal takes the bait, the trap is triggered, permanently ensnaring it.

Offenses and other distractions are the literal bait of Satan. Many believers in the body of Christ are being distracted by hurts, disappointments, and offenses—all of them devices the enemy has set as a trap for their very soul. His whole agenda is to permanently ensnare the believer in destructive life patterns. But the apostle Paul went on to say, *"The God of peace shall bruise Satan under your feet shortly"* (Romans 16:20). He was reminding the church in Rome that God would ultimately crush Satan and his schemes, the implication being that they need not become preoccupied with the devil's antics but should instead focus on praise, worship, and thanksgiving to God for His goodness. One of the best ways to overcome spiritual distraction in your life is worship your heavenly Father.

WORSHIP IS ONE OF THE MOST POWERFUL WEAPONS IN SPIRITUAL WARFARE BECAUSE IT TAKES OUR ATTENTION OFF OUR CIRCUMSTANCES AND PLACES IT ON GOD.

The Bible says, "*Thou wilt keep him in perfect peace, whose mind is stayed on thee: because he trusteth in thee*" (Isaiah 26:3). This is a very powerful spiritual principle. The more we learn to focus on the Lord rather than on the enemy's activity, the more we sap the devil of his power over us. Remember, Satan loves attention. He is extremely self-centered and egotistical. This is why he loves to get believers to focus on themselves. The goal of the devil is to produce so much noise and chaos in the life of the believer that he or she will no longer hear the still, small voice of God (see 1 Kings 19:12), which leads them into victory and breakthrough. Refuse to be distracted! Set your sights on God through praise and worship, and ignore the enemy when he tries to distract you.

4. Oppression

Now about that time Herod the king stretched forth his hands to vex certain of the church. (Acts 12:1)

If the enemy cannot successfully tempt, deceive, or distract a believer, his fourth and final strategy is to oppress. As we mentioned before, oppression involves the persecution, affliction, control, and abuse of a person in his or her thoughts, emotions, or physical body. This oppression can come in the form of sexual addiction, sickness, fear, intimidation, bitterness, discouragement, or any other life-controlling issue.

The Bible records in the twelfth chapter of Acts how King Herod "*stretched forth his hand to vex certain* [people in] *the church.*" The word "*vex*" comes from the Greek word *kakoō*—to oppress, afflict, harm, maltreat, or embitter. The disciples of Jesus had been proclaiming the gospel of the kingdom, and King Herod intended to silence them by means of oppression and persecution.

Satan acts with the same agenda as Herod did. Remember, the devil is a spiritual antagonist whose sole purpose is to prevent you and me from advancing the kingdom of God in our lives and in the world around us. Herod was specifically targeting key influencers in the church because he knew that their imprisonment would discourage the other believers. And Satan does the same thing today. Beloved, rest assured that if the enemy is coming against you aggressively, it is because you have great influence in the kingdom.

OPPRESSION IS DESIGNED TO DISCOURAGE AND HINDER GOD'S PEOPLE FROM MOVING FORWARD IN HIS KINGDOM PURPOSES.

There are many people in the church who are being persecuted by the devil. He has them trapped in a physiological prison of fear, bitterness, addiction, and despondency. The key to overcoming persecution is to recognize where it comes from. If the nature of your struggle is that of chaos or confusion, you can be sure that it originates from Satan, for the Bible says that God is not the author of confusion but of peace. (See 1 Corinthians 14:33.)

Earlier, I introduced the term "demonization." By this, I do not mean possession by a demon but *oppression* by a demon, or a disembodied evil spirit. Any believer who allows demonic forces to work unhindered in his or her body or soul for a prolonged period of time is, in fact, demonized. I have spoken with Christian believers who found it extremely difficult to carry out even the most basic of spiritual disciplines, such as attending church or praying, and I believe that demonic oppression is to blame. Remember, demonic oppression stems from Satan's desire to hinder the advance of the kingdom of God. For this reason, the more you seek to pursue the purposes of God and His kingdom, the more spiritual opposition you will face.

Keep in mind, however, that some demonic oppression does not come from obeying God but from opening the door to demons through willful sin and disobedience. I have counseled countless believers who are suffering unnecessarily because they have yet to surrender their lives completely to the lordship of Jesus. As a result, they have given the devil and his demons a legal right to oppress their mind, will, and emotions. Later, we will talk about how demons enter, and how to close the door to them.

Winning the Battle Within

Using the Scriptures, we have explored the four strategies the enemy uses to hinder believers: temptation, deception, distraction, and oppression. Every spiritual battle that we face typically falls into one of the aforementioned categories. Now that you know the enemies mode of operation, you should be better equipped in dealing with the spiritual opposition that you face.

As mentioned earlier, the real battle that we face is an internal battle—a struggle that rages in the mind of every believer. Whether you are facing discouragement, fear, anxiety, abandonment, rejection, or another type of emotional distress, you must understand that these are simply weapons that the devil uses in an effort to get you to believe wrongly. He knows that a wrong belief system will produce wrong choices, and consistent wrong choices will lead to wrong living. The enemy desires for you and me to surrender our birthright to him and ultimately abort our destiny.

On the other hand, right believing equates to right living. I don't know about you, but I refuse to give the enemy one more inch of my life. Many people are suffering silently. They are facing internal chaos and don't know what to do. Oftentimes, people settle for simply pretending to be free, forever missing out on enjoying the real freedom that God has made available to them through His Son and by His Word. Let's not be among them!

Renew Your Mind

Mind renewal is a vital means to experiencing lasting change and transformation. This internal renovation is key to winning the battle against the enemy of our souls.

In the following verse, the apostle Paul exhorted us as follows:

Be not conformed to this world: but be ye transformed by the renewing of your mind, that ye may prove what is that good, and acceptable, and perfect, will of God. (Romans 12:2)

The first step in renewing the mind is to adopt a self-image that aligns with the Word of God. In other words, you must stop accepting as "normal" the issue or sin that you have been struggling with. Anxiety attacks are not normal. Waking up in a pool of sweat is not normal. Sickness and infirmity are not normal. You must accept a new normal! That is, you must accept the new life that Christ has made available to you by the Holy Spirit. This life can be lived and demonstrated only when we have undergone a supernatural renewal of our mind. The phrase *"renewing of your mind"* comes from the Greek word *anakainōsis*, which essentially means a complete change for the better.

Decide That Enough Is Enough!

At some point in your life, you must draw a line in the sand, as I did, and tell the devil that he has no more place in your thoughts, your emotions, or your physical body. You may be dealing with an addiction, struggling with lustful thoughts, battling a chronic illness, or feeling bound by discouragement. I have good news for you: You can be free!

That dark presence in my room was nothing more than the intimidating hand of the devil, attempting to oppress me and silence me. When I figured that out, I decided that enough was enough. I recognized that *"the name of the* Lord *is a strong tower:*

the righteous runneth into it, and is safe" (Proverbs 18:10). The name of Jesus is more powerful than the devil's entire arsenal. The name of Jesus is your greatest weapon against the enemy. Once you realize the magnitude of your weapon in comparison to the devil, you will soon gain the upper hand in this battle you wage from within.

Deliverance Prayer

Father, I thank You that Your Word exposes the strategies and tactics of the devil. I recognize that the enemy of my soul utilizes temptation, deception, distraction, and oppression to bring the people of God into bondage. Right now, I declare that I will not yield to his devices, and that I will yield only to the leading and guiding of the Holy Spirit.

Right now, I expose my entire spirit, soul, and body to the blood of Jesus Christ, the Word of God, and to the fire of the Holy Spirit; and I command anything operating in my soul that was not planted by the Lord Jesus Christ to be uprooted, in Jesus' name! I declare that guilt, shame, and defeat have no more dominion over my mind. I am free to worship and serve the true, living God in spirit and in truth. Thank You, Lord, for Your great deliverance in my life, in Jesus' name. Amen!

DARKNESS DEFINED

*He brought them out of darkness and the shadow of death,
and brake their bands in sunder.*
—Psalm 107:14

Thus far, I have used the term "darkness" quite frequently. I mentioned previously that Satan is the ruler of *"the darkness of this world"* (Ephesians 6:12), and that this realm specifically comprises spiritual blindness or ignorance. However, in the Old Testament, darkness takes on a slightly different meaning.

Its first mention occurs in the creation account:

And the earth was without form, and void; and darkness was upon the face of the deep. And the Spirit of God moved upon the face of the waters. (Genesis 1:2)

As we look at this passage from a Hebraic perspective, it will give us an even greater insight into what darkness really is. The Hebrew word used for *"darkness"* in this verse is *choshek*, which means "obscurity." Here, darkness is not expressed as a state of mind but as a physical place, or, more accurately, a realm—a kingdom or territory over which a sovereign rules.

The creation account continues as follows:

> And God said, Let there be light: and there was light. And God saw the light, that it was good: and God divided the light from the darkness. (Genesis 1:3–4)

According to the Law of First Mention, it is important that we notice what God did in the beginning as it relates to both the light and the darkness. The Bible says that God did two very significant things: (1) He blessed the light and declared it good, and (2) He separated the light from the darkness. The phrase *"God saw the light, that it was good"* is an idiomatic expression of favor, blessing, and endearment. In other words, the author of Genesis is telling us that God preferred the light to the darkness because it was of a higher and better nature.

The next thing that God did was make an apparent distinction between the two realms: the realm of light (where He rules) and the realm of darkness (where Satan and his demons rule). I believe that this distinction was a prophetic symbol of spiritual warfare. There is a realm called "darkness" that God has called us out of, as we read in Peter's first epistle:

> Ye are a chosen generation, a royal priesthood, an holy nation, a peculiar people; that ye should shew forth the praises of him who **hath called you out of darkness into his marvellous light**. (1 Peter 2:9)

GOD HAS MADE AN ETERNAL DISTINCTION BETWEEN THE REALM OF LIGHT AND THE REALM OF DARKNESS. THROUGH JESUS, WE HAVE BEEN GIVEN RULE OVER THE DARKNESS.

Beloved, God was telling us from the very beginning of creation that there are two distinct spiritual kingdoms: the kingdom of light and the kingdom of darkness. Again, when we use the term "darkness" in this book, we are talking about Satan's kingdom, which is ruled and operated by spiritual wickedness, evil, chaos, and confusion. We are referring to the realm of the demonic. But through the power of the Word of God, you can live in victory over this kingdom and put it under your feet.

A Clash of Two Kingdoms

Whatever your race, culture, nationality, education, social status, or other demographic detail, it doesn't matter; the realm of darkness does not discriminate in its endeavor to attack the children of God. There is no denying that there is such a thing called evil in this world. The enemy of our soul is working tirelessly behind the veil of this natural realm to inflict calamity and destruction on anyone—young and old, poor and rich, male and female—who will yield to his insidious attacks.

The moment you were born again, you became a citizen of the kingdom of God and, by default, an enemy of Satan's kingdom—the realm of darkness. This realm is responsible for wars, violence, murder, corruption, sexual perversion, failed marriages, immorality, addictions, and any other malevolent forces at work on the earth today. Granted, human responsibility and free will play a part in these evils, as well; but I am simply bringing to your attention a little-known truth: The devil is very real, and he operates in the unseen realm. Unseen oppressors are abusing millions of people all over the world, and I believe it is time for this unjust abuse to come to an end. I believe that those of us who know the truth can put a stop to the tyrannical reign of the evil one, not only in our lives, but also in the lives of our loved ones, our neighbors, our coworkers, and so forth.

GOD'S KINGDOM HAS ALWAYS BEEN, AND WILL ALWAYS BE, MORE POWERFUL THAN THE DEVIL'S KINGDOM.

Since the beginning of creation, there has been a cataclysmic struggle going on between the kingdom of light—God's kingdom—and the kingdom of darkness. Jesus was well aware of the existence of both kingdoms and their operations during His earthly ministry, for He had frequent contact with the kingdom of darkness as He cast demons out of people and commanded those with physical ailments to become well.

One scene worth studying is recorded in the eighth chapter of Matthew. Jesus had just come into the country of Gergesenes when He encountered two demon-possessed men. The moment these men saw Jesus, *"they cried out, saying, What have we to do with thee, Jesus, thou Son of God? art thou come hither to torment us before the time?"* (Matthew 8:29). Why did the demons cry out when they met Him? Because Jesus literally "tormented" them. The word *"torment"* in this passage comes from the Greek word *basanizō*, which means to question by applying torture.

Notice that they referred to Him as the *"Son of God."* In other words, they were acknowledging the realm He represented, which was the kingdom of God. The moment the kingdom of God encountered the kingdom of darkness, there was a spiritual collision. Whenever two objects collide, collateral damage always occurs—and the kingdom of God always prevails against the kingdom of darkness. This is why, wherever Jesus went, blind eyes were opened, the sick were healed, and the lame walked. He was on a "demolition mission" to destroy the infrastructure of Satan's kingdom (i.e., sickness, depression, and death). The Bible says, *"For this purpose the Son of God was manifested, that he might* **destroy** *the works of the devil*" (1 John 3:8). "*Destroy*" is another word for "demolish." Wherever Jesus encountered the devil's handiwork, He demolished that work and rendered his agents powerless.

You have the legal right and authority to do the same thing Jesus did. When you encounter demons, they should be begging for mercy. Why? Because you are a king and a priest. The secret to victory is knowing which kingdom you belong to.

Identifying the Strong Man

I want you to picture the most hardened criminal you could possibly conceive of. Now, imagine that this criminal has broken into your home, stolen your goods, and abducted your family, and is currently holding them hostage in a gated compound. What will you do? For most of us, the answer goes without saying! We will use whatever means necessary to rescue our precious loved ones from the hands of this evil menace.

Beloved, Satan is that criminal! He is a menace to society, a hardened madman who is set on taking from you that which you hold dear. He is a thief and a robber with no remorse or compassion. As with most hardened criminals, the only thing that the devil will respond to is brute force. He must be confronted. And, like it or not, this confrontation with the realm of darkness is not optional. The battle began long before you and I were ever born. Remember, Satan was a murderer from the very beginning. (See John 8:44.) Because this is the case, harmony with him is impossible. We cannot coexist peacefully with the enemy.

The devil has declared war against the body of Christ, and if he had it his way, he would take no prisoners. Fortunately for you and me, Jesus has already defeated the enemy. And now it's up to us to reinforce that defeat by taking authority over him.

In a parable He related in the eleventh chapter of Luke, Jesus gave us a picture of how it looks when we take down the devil:

> *When a strong man armed keepeth his palace, his goods are in peace: but when a stronger than he shall come upon him, and overcome him, he taketh from him all his armor wherein he trusted, and divideth his spoils.* (Luke 11:21–22)

The enemy of your soul stands as a "strong man" blocking the door to your freedom, breakthrough, and healing. He has captured your dreams, stolen your vision, and hijacked your destiny. He will not let go of your stuff until someone stronger than he forces him release it. Good news—Jesus is stronger than the devil! In fact, the Bible says that we have already overcome the evil one, because greater is He who lives in us than He that lives in the world. (See 1 John 4:4.) Through the power of the greater One, we can conquer the enemy.

THE GREATER ONE WHO LIVES INSIDE YOU HAS ALREADY OVERCOME THE FORCES OF DARKNESS. JESUS IS STRONGER THAN THE STRONG MAN, SATAN.

The Bible says that we can "divide the enemy's spoils." The word *"spoils"* comes from the Greek word *skulon*, which means "booty," or the weapons and valuables stripped off a defeated enemy. Every time you confront the realm of darkness head-on, you strip the enemy of his weapons. The more you confront him, the weaker he will become. Most believers don't know this, and, as a result, they are afraid to confront the demonic activity operating in their lives. We must stand up and fight!

The Enemy Known as Jezebel

When my wife and I started our church, we had no clue what we were doing. Let me explain! We knew theology, we had some practical ministry experience, and we were anointed, but we were completely unaware of the intense spiritual battle that was involved in planting a church. You must understand that Satan hates the church, especially the local church. For him, the local church represents the most powerful evangelistic organism on the planet.

On this point, I would have to agree with the devil. There is nothing more effective in winning the lost than the Spirit-filled, life-giving local church. This is why the devil attacks the local church with such intensity. In addition to the fact that we were a brand-new church, we were also a prophetic church that proclaimed the gospel of Jesus Christ with signs and wonders following. And if there is one thing that prophetic churches attract, it is the spirit of Jezebel.

The Jezebel spirit is named after Jezebel, a false prophetess in the Old Testament who was also the wife of King Ahab. (See 1 Kings 16:30–31.) Jezebel was responsible for seducing ancient Israel into the worship of Baal, an ancient Phoenician fertility god, whom the people venerated through acts of sexual immorality. Jezebel's reign in Israel was characterized by manipulation, seduction, intimidation, and control. However, there was one barrier to Jezebel's evils scheme: the prophet Elijah. He proclaimed the uncompromising Word of God and slew the prophets of Baal (see 1 Kings 18:40), provoking the wrath of Queen Jezebel to rage against him.

THE SPIRIT OF JEZEBEL SEEKS TO CUT OFF THE FLOW OF THE PROPHETIC AND DRAW PEOPLE AWAY INTO IDOLATRY AND IMMORALITY.

In Revelation 2:20, John recorded God's reproof of the church at Thyatira because of the idolatry and sexual immorality they had been practicing:

> Notwithstanding I have a few things against thee, because thou sufferest that woman Jezebel, which calleth herself a prophetess, to teach and to seduce my servants to commit fornication, and to eat things sacrificed unto idols.

In this statement, God was not referring to the natural Queen Jezebel but to the demonic spirit of Jezebel. The word *"seduce"* in this verse comes from the Greek word *planaō*—to lead away from the truth; to lead into error; to deceive. This evil spirit was luring the leadership of the church into error and false doctrine.

Jezebel is the spirit behind pornography, sexual perversion, adultery, homosexuality, lesbianism, and the seduction of spiritual leaders. I have witnessed this spirit operate through vessels formerly yielded to Christ, causing chaos and confusion in churches, ministries, and marriages. It is important to note that although the person for whom it is named was a woman, and although it is often personified as such, the Jezebel spirit is gender neutral.

Like all demonic spirits, the Jezebel spirit has as her goal to bring believers into absolute bondage. There are countless churches and pastors who are bound by this demonic force. Unfortunately, many of them have no idea that they are under satanic oppression. They think that they are simply dealing with normal lust, discouragement, and fear. The devil is a convincing liar!

Unmasking the Spirit of Jezebel

Years ago, we had a firsthand encounter with the Jezebel spirit. As a young, inexperienced pastor, I was always excited to meet new people and to forge new relationships. Every person who walked through the doors of our church was a leader in the making, in my opinion. One day, someone walked through the door carrying much more than I could have imagined. He was charismatic, charming, and intelligent. He said all the right things and appeared to be everything we were looking for in a church member. He quickly assimilated into the church community and made himself readily available to meet any needs that arose. Anytime we hosted a church event, he was present. Whenever we organized a prayer meeting, he was there. As you can imagine, I was extremely happy to meet someone who caught the vision of the church so quickly—or so I thought.

Gradually, the Lord made me aware that there was something seriously wrong with the situation. The more this person sought to gain my trust, the more uncomfortable I became. However, we were in need of all the help we could get, so I ignored the warning signs and continued to move forward. After several months, I noticed that this individual was becoming increasingly vocal about his differences of opinion regarding the way we ran our ministry. He would disagree with the way we conducted outreach, raised funds, lead worship, and even advertised the church. And he began holding secret meetings with many of the leaders of the church.

My wife had received several warnings about this particular person in her dreams, but it was if a cloak was covering our eyes.

THE JEZEBEL SPIRIT IS A MANIFESTATION OF THE SPIRIT OF OPPRESSION.

Charm turned into deception, and the secret meetings became a vehicle for slander and division in the church. My leadership was being undermined before my eyes, yet there seemed to be nothing I could do about it. I confronted this person on several occasions, but each time, he denied any wrongdoing. When I would attempt to address the issue with other people in the church, they didn't seem to have any clue what I was talking about.

Like yeast spreads through bread dough, the dishonor, though seemingly small, began to spread throughout the entire church.

This attack was insidious! People started to come under physical oppression as this malevolent force worked through the least unsuspecting vessels. My wife and I began arguing frequently. I was being attacked in my mind with lustful thoughts. We were experiencing unexplained lack and stagnation in our finances. Our children were suffering continual sickness. Both the church and my marriage were being torn apart, and I felt helpless to save either one.

So, I did the only thing that I knew to do: I prayed. It was while I was in prayer that the Holy Spirit revealed to me that I was dealing with the spirit of Jezebel—a spirit of witchcraft, deception, and control. Like Queen Jezebel of the Old Testament, this demonic spirit was trying to silence our prophetic voice. The devil knew that our church was capable of tearing down his kingdom, so he attempted to destroy us in our infancy. Unfortunately for him, I have never been one to roll over and play dead! When the Holy Spirit removed the veil from my eyes so that I could see clearly, I recognized that I was not wrestling against flesh and blood but against the very powers of darkness. I knew that it was time to confront this evil and break its grip, once and for all!

Breaking the Spirit of Oppression

At some point, I decided that enough was enough! No longer would I tolerate the oppressive hand of Jezebel in my mind, marriage, and ministry. But my question was, "How am I going to deal with this spirit?"

A Scripture that spoke to me during this time was 2 Kings 9:7:

> *And thou shalt smite the house of Ahab thy master, that I may avenge the blood of my servants the prophets, and the blood of all the servants of the Lord, at the hand of Jezebel.*

The word *"smite"* comes from the Hebrew word *nakah*, which means to "strike," "wound," "slaughter," or "slay." In this verse, God was calling Elijah to destroy the oppressive system of King Ahab and bring Jezebel's evil reign to an end so that Israel would be able to worship the living God once again. And I realized that He was calling me to do the same thing! He wanted me to take back my marriage and ministry from the murderous grip of Satan.

Through the Jezebel spirit, the devil had ushered in to my church and marriage a spirit of oppression and witchcraft, which is the employment of evil spirits to manipulate or otherwise control another person. Through rebellion, slander, and seduction, I had unknowingly been brought under ungodly control. Now it was time to break free! I decided to confront the person responsible for the turmoil in our church—more precisely, the spirit operating within him—and tell him that he would no longer be able to operate in rebellion against the church leadership or to cause strife and division in the church.

The moment I did this, a spiritual battle ensued. Late that night, while I was lying in bed, my wife woke up, screaming, "What did you do?" I had not spoken to her about my confrontation, so I asked her what she meant. She told me that she had seen the very person I had just confronted, standing in our bedroom in the form of a black panther. Immediately, fear gripped my heart.

JEZEBEL OPERATES THROUGH REBELLION, SORCERY, MANIPULATION, AND CONTROL.

Several days later, I was awakened by a dark presence late at night. I couldn't breathe! My chest became tight, and I felt as if I was having a heart attack. The more I struggled, the more I sank into the darkness. Every time I tried to speak, no words would come out. I was dying, and I knew, by the Holy Spirit, that if I didn't fight back, the devil would end my life.

Then this truth came to mind: *Greater is He who lives in me!* (See 1 John 4:4.) From the deepest recesses of my spirit, I screamed these words: "I bind you, spirit of oppression, in the name of Jesus!"

All of a sudden, there was a release. I could breathe again. Panting heavily, I saw what I had previously missed. Hovering over me was an eight-foot translucent being that resembled an octopus, having eight long tentacles. It was almost as if the spirit was confused because I had recognized it, because, in a matter of moments, the spirit vanished completely.

What happened in that moment? I was literally attack by a spirit of oppression. The confrontation with the spirit of Jezebel was a Trojan horse meant to open the gates to oppression and even death. The attack in my sleep was simply a manifestation of the spirit that had been assigned to destroy my ministry all along. Through the name and authority of Jesus, I broke the power of that oppressive spirit. Eventually, that spirit oppression and the persons hosting it were forced out of our midst by the power of the Holy Spirit. You have the same authority inside you to break free from oppression—permanently.

Exercising Your Spiritual Senses

If you and I are going to walk in victory over the forces of darkness, it is critical that we learn to discern the various spirits at work in the world around us. Among the spiritual gifts listed in 1 Corinthians 12:8–10 is one known as *"discerning of spirits."* What does this gift entail, exactly? The word *"discerning"* comes from the Greek word *diakrisis*—a distinguishing or judging. To distinguish means to recognize the difference between two things. In other words, the gift of the discerning of spirits is the ability to distinguish between various demonic spirits, as well as to recognize angelic beings.

In the case of the story I shared about the spirit of Jezebel operating in our church, we discerned that the person I described was operating in a spirit of manipulation and control—a spirit so subtle, it went unrecognized for a while. From the outside, everything seemed normal. But discernment enables us to perceive the unseen realm. It gives us the supernatural ability to distinguish the invisible forces at work in any given situation or circumstance. And it is this gift that finally showed us what was really going on under our noses.

It is important to note that there is no such gift as the "discerning of people." Judging other people is actually a sin, because judgment is a job that's meant for God alone. (See, for example, Hebrews 10:30.) The Holy Spirit grants to certain individuals the ability to discern the *spirits at work within* other people, for the purpose of their deliverance and restoration. We must be cautious in how we approach other people, and make sure that we are not operating in a critical spirit but with an attitude of love and compassion.

THE DISCERNMENT OF SPIRITS ENABLES THE BELIEVER TO SEE INTO THE INVISIBLE REALM AND DISTINGUISH GOOD FROM EVIL, LIGHT FROM DARKNESS.

Made to See by the Holy Spirit

Satan's kingdom is invisible, which means that we must exercise discernment if we are to recognize his clandestine activity. For that reason, the Holy Spirit is our most valuable resource when it comes to spiritual warfare and deliverance—He alone will open our eyes in the spiritual realm and give us the internal knowing that we need in order to identify and neutralize the powers of darkness.

This is why getting to know the Holy Spirit is such a critical component to living a victorious Christian life. You may never have encountered a Jezebel spirit or faced a spirit of oppression in the way I described, but that doesn't change the fact that there is a realm of darkness that seeks to conquer your life. Many times, the malevolent forces of Satan are so subtle that we don't notice or recognize them.

The more we exercise our spiritual senses, the better we will be able to discern the unseen realm. Just as we must exercise our natural senses (touch, taste, smell, hearing, and sight), we must also learn to develop and strengthen our spiritual senses. The Bible says, "*Strong meat belongeth to them that are of full age, even those who by reason of use have their **senses exercised** to discern both good and evil*" (Hebrews 5:14). It is "*by reason of use*" that our spiritual senses are exercised and honed. In other words, we have to practice the discerning of spirits in order to become proficient at it. The word "*exercised*" in this verse is the word *gumnazō*, which refers to vigorous exercise or training. It is where we get the English word *gymnasium*. The Word of God is your gym, and prayer is your exercise!

Deliverance Prayer

Father, in the name of Jesus, I take authority over the demonic spirit of oppression, in Jesus' name. I command all fear, manipulation, intimidation, and dread to go from me right now, in Jesus' name. I am a child of God, entitled to all of the rights and privileges that belong to every citizen of the kingdom of God, and I declare that any and all demonic attacks on my mind, emotions, and/or health must cease and desist—right now. I hereby commit to exercising my sense of spiritual discernment, that I might expose the devil's schemes.

I command the spirit of Jezebel and all her cohorts—including rebellion, idolatry, lust, pornography, adultery, sexual immorality, depression, and premature death—to leave me and the people I am interceding for right now. I submit myself to the lordship of Jesus, and I declare that He alone is my King and Deliverer. Thank You, Lord, for setting me free through Your supernatural power. In Jesus' name, amen!

EXPOSING THE ENEMY

He sitteth in the lurking places of the villages: in the secret places doth he murder the innocent.
—Psalm 10:8

Many years ago, a friend of our family told us that she had been struggling with nightmares for a very long time. She was a leader in his local congregation who was knowledgeable of the Bible and spiritually mature, yet she had a deep, dark secret. Every night, she was being tormented by horrible dreams that were so frightening, she was afraid to go to bed.

One day, after coming to the end of herself, she cried out to God. "Lord, please deliver me from these demonic dreams," she prayed.

The situation seemed hopeless until, one night, after a time of fasting and prayer, something unusual happened. In the middle of the night, our friend sat up in bed and noticed that her body was still lying down on the mattress. She was having an out-of-body experience. When she looked forward, she saw a grotesque creature resembling a troll. According to her, this figure was translucent, just like the one I described earlier. And, similar to my experience, this demonic creature seemed shocked that it was no longer invisible.

Suddenly, the spirit jumped off of our friend and retreated to one corner of the room. Great boldness rose up in her spirit as she looked to her side and saw a long sword attached to her waist. She stood up, took the sword from its sheath, and cut this demonic spirit into pieces. When she came out of this open vision, all traces of fear and terror were completely gone.

Since that episode, she has not been terrorized by a single nightmare—praise the Lord Jesus! I share this story with you to bring out the fact that we cannot fight an enemy we do not see. Even though this woman was a well-meaning Christian, she could not overcome the oppressive hand of the enemy until he was exposed. The Holy Spirit opened her eyes and allowed her to see the demonic spirit behind her gruesome nightmares. Once she saw what she was dealing with, the power of the darkness was broken. God is about to expose the enemy in your life today! Once the devil has been exposed, he loses his power over you.

YOU CANNOT SUCCESSFULLY DEFEAT AN ENEMY YOU DO NOT SEE! OPEN YOUR SPIRITUAL EYES AND TAKE AUTHORITY OVER THE EVIL ONE.

Just like my friend, many people are harboring a deep, dark secret. They are engaged in a secret battle. They are pastors, elders, Sunday school teachers, and stay-at-home moms. As I said before, the enemy of your soul does not discriminate. I believe that the Holy Spirit is about to open your spiritual eyes to let you see that the thing you are battling is not just a "normal" struggle but a clandestine attempt of the prince of darkness to keep you bound and afraid.

The Bible says that the enemy of your soul sits in the *"lurking places"* (Psalm 10:8). This phrase comes from the Hebrew word *ma'arab*, which means to "lie in ambush." An ambush is a surprise attack by someone who lies in wait in a concealed position. So, you can see that the power of the enemy is in his concealment. Satan does not want you to recognize or discern his activity in your life. In fact, the devil loves anonymity. That is why it is of great importance that we refuse to remain in the dark when it comes to the battles that we face. If you are suffering from nightmares, anxiety attacks, or fears, bring them into the light!

Now You See Me; Now You Don't!

In the early 1900s, there came on the scene a very famous illusionist by the name of Harry Houdini. He was well-known for his escape routines and handcuff tricks. Later on in his career, his act evolved to include death-defying stunts and large-scale illusions. One of his most famous illusions was called the "Vanishing Elephant." This illusion was first performed on January 7, 1918, at the New York Hippodrome. The goal of the illusion was to cause an elephant—eight feet tall and weighing five tons—to disappear before a live audience of five thousand.

During the act, Houdini walked an elephant into an eight-foot-square cabinet and closed the door after it. When he reopened the cabinet door, the elephant was no longer visible. It had vanished! Or had it? In truth, the elephant had been in the cabinet all along; it was merely concealed by an optical illusion created by special curtains housed within the cabinet doors. This was nothing more than expert sleight of hand and the manipulation of viewing angles.

Like a master magician, Satan is an illusionist who he loves to conceal his plans behind the curtains of darkness and ignorance. Many people are harboring "elephants" in their closets and don't even know it. These "elephants" take the form of fear, lust, hurt, anger, anxiety, and depression. But remember, the enemy's power is nothing more than an illusion—a deceptive appearance or impression—energized by fear and ignorance. The moment you see through his spiritual "disappearing acts," his power is broken off your life, once and for all.

YOU MUST UNDERSTAND THAT SATAN'S POWER IS NOTHING MORE THAN AN ILLUSION.

The devil wants you and me to believe that the challenges we face in our lives are normal, unchangeable realities. I recently had a conversation with a woman who believed that the anxiety attacks she'd been experiencing were a "gift" from God, intended to keep her humble and help her to empathize with other people. Beloved, this type of thinking comes straight from the pit of Hades! The enemy has deceived this woman, and others like her, into believing that something evil is actually good.

Such an act is fitting for an evil being who masquerades as something good. *"And no marvel; for Satan himself is transformed into an angel of light"* (2 Corinthians 11:14). The word *"transformed"* comes from the Greek word *metaschēmatizō*, which means "to transfigure." In other words, the devil changes his appearance based on his evil agenda. He may take the form of sickness or depression, or even in something positive; but make no mistakes—he's still the devil.

Just like the illusionist trick that we mentioned earlier, the enemy seeks to hide himself behind the veil of invisibility. We must expose him by the power of God's Word!

In the sixteenth chapter of Acts, Luke gave us a great example of what I'm talking about. The story starts out like this:

> *And it came to pass, as we went to prayer, a certain damsel possessed with a spirit of divination met us, which brought her*

masters much gain by soothsaying: the same followed Paul and us, and cried, saying, These men are the servants of the most high God, which shew unto us the way of salvation. And this did she many days. (Acts 16:16–18)

This woman sounds innocent enough—after all, she acknowledged that Paul and the others were servants of the Most High God. But watch what happens next:

But Paul, being grieved, turned and said to the spirit, I command thee in the name of Jesus Christ to come out of her. And he came out the same hour. (Acts 16:18–19)

Wait a minute! Paul cast a spirit out of her? Why? Wasn't she speaking the truth? Not entirely. Paul had acute spiritual discernment, which allowed him to distinguish whether something originated with God or whether it originated with the devil. Beloved, you need that same level of discernment to see through the illusions of the kingdom of darkness.

Recognizing the Spirit of Python

The young woman in the scene we just studied was possessed by a *"spirit of divination"* (Acts 16:16). To the untrained believer, this may seem like a plain and simple statement; however, upon further examination, this Scripture uncovers the source behind the oppression of many believers in the body of Christ. What is the spirit of divination? And why does the Bible draw specific attention to this spirit in the book of Acts?

The word *"divination"* in the above passage comes from the Greek word *Puthon*, which literally means "python" (serpent) or dragon. The term refers specifically to the Pythian serpent of Greek mythology, which dwelled in the region of Pytho. This spirit was actually worshipped as a deity.

In other words, this damsel was possessed with a spirit of python. As you probably know, a python is a heavy-bodied snake that kills its victims by constriction. Just like the physical python, the spirit of python chokes its victims to death. This is the spirit responsible for addictions to pornography and alcohol, for depression, for suicide, for mental illness, and for failed marriages.

Pythons are known for camouflaging themselves in their tropical habitat, a method of concealment that allows them to strike their victims without warning. In the same manner, the spirit of python conceals itself through pleasure. Did you know that there is a high price to pay for indulging in ungodly pleasures? Beloved, do not allow the spirit of python to draw you into bondage. How can you tell when a spirit of python is operating? Usually, a python spirit is evident when there is a pervasive, life-controlling issue at work in the mind, soul, or physical body, often in the form of an addiction, a chronic illness, or a mental stronghold.

THE SPIRIT OF PYTHON IS A SPIRIT OF ADDICTION, DEPRESSION, AND CHRONIC FEAR.

How does one break the power of a python spirit? First, you must recognize that you are dealing with a demonic entity. So often, we have the tendency to rationalize the things we are struggling with and to attribute them to a non-spiritual source, such as personality or environment, when, in fact, we are dealing with a demonic spirit. The moment you recognize and identify the python spirit, its grip on your mind and soul is loosened.

The next step is to do what the apostle Paul did in Acts 16:18: *"But Paul, being grieved, turned and said to the spirit, I command thee in the name of Jesus Christ to come out of her."* He was tired of being tormented by this foul spirit, so he spoke to it with authority and commanded it to leave.

You and I have to speak to the spirit of oppression and command it to leave, in Jesus' name. We have to exercise the name and authority of Jesus to break the power of sin, addiction, and bondage in our lives. You may be thinking, *It can't be that easy!* My friend, it *is* that easy, because Jesus Christ has already paid the price for your freedom and deliverance. You simply need to lay claim to the victory He has won for you.

Now is the time for the grip of the python spirit to be broken. No longer can he hide behind your ignorance, because the fire of God is burning up his camouflage as we speak. I declare that from this day forward, you are free from all life-controlling issues, in Jesus' name!

How Demons Enter

If we are going to expose the enemy in our lives and secure the victory in spiritual warfare and deliverance, we must first gain a basic understanding of how demonic spirits operate and gain access to our lives. The question remains, If demons have the ability to oppress believers, how do they enter their life? Remember, there is a difference between oppression and possession. A nonbeliever has no defense against the powers of darkness; therefore, demons can enter and manipulate him at will. This is not the case for the born-again believer.

There are four primary ways in which demonic spirits enter the lives of believers, and they are: (1) unrepentant sin, (2) generational curses, (3) ungodly soul ties, and (4) involvement in the occult.

1. Unrepentant Sin

> *My little children, these things write I unto you, that ye sin not. And if any man sin, we have an advocate with the Father, Jesus Christ the righteous. And he is the propitiation for our sins: and not for ours only, but also for the sins of the whole world.* (1 John 2:1–2)

Whether people want to accept it or not, God expects all His children to live a life of righteousness and moral purity. However, God knows that you and I will make mistakes from time to time, as a result of our humanity, which is innately sinful. This is why the Bible says that we have an Advocate (the Lord Jesus Christ) who makes intercession for us and represents us before the Father. His blood is the eternal propitiatory sacrifice for all our sins—past, present, and future.

The Bible says, *"He that committeth sin is of the devil; for the devil sinneth from the beginning"* (1 John 3:8). The word for *"sin"* here is the Greek word *hamartanō*, which means "to miss the mark," or to wander from the path. In context, the author, John, was talking about a consistent deviation from God's Word, or a habitual practice of sin. The Bible says that if we are born again, we should no longer make a regular practice of willfully sinning against God. Willful sin can open the door to demonic oppression in a believer's life. Why? Because sin is the nature of Satan, as well as the atmosphere in which he has a legal right to operate.

Therefore, whenever we do "miss the mark" by sinning, it is crucial that we confess our sin and repent of it before God, who is quick to forgive and abounding in mercy. Proverbs 28:13 assures us, *"He that covereth his sins shall not prosper: but whoso confesseth and forsaketh them shall have mercy."*

You have probably heard the expression "skeletons in the closet." This simply means that there are secrets or shameful events in the past that people choose to cover up rather than bring to the light. Almost every family has "skeletons in the closet." These secrets can range from an adulterous affair, to gambling, to addictions, to homosexuality, to molestation, to incest—and beyond. Earlier, we discussed how the enemy of our soul conceals himself in the darkness. Whenever there are secret sins in our marriages, families, churches, and communities, there is often a cesspool of demonic activity. Unfortunately, we live in a culture that is obsessed with appearances. People would rather look the part than experience true freedom. Anytime we cover up our sins or iniquities, the devil uses those very secret sins to condemn and oppress us.

However, as it says in Proverbs 28:13, we will never prosper as long as we are covering up or concealing our sins. The word *"prosper"* in this verse comes from the Hebrew word *tsalach*—to advance or make progress. If we attempt to conceal our iniquities, sins, and shortcomings, our spiritual life will stagnate, with no evidence of growth or flourishing. But the moment we confess our sins to God and forsake them is the moment we experience freedom and victory in our lives.

This doesn't mean that you should dig up every secret sin in your family or confess to each person you meet every dark deed you've ever done. It means that you should walk deliberately and consistently in the light of God's Word. Whenever the Holy Spirit convicts you of a sinful area in your life, you should repent immediately and renounce that particular sin or issue. Developing the habit of exposing your heart before the Holy Spirit will empower you to live a consistent life of freedom and victory.

2. Generational Curses

Throughout the Bible, we see generational curses at work in the lives of specific individuals and groups of people. Generational curses are the consequence of a failure to heed such warnings as God issued in the book of Deuteronomy and Exodus—for example, Exodus 34:6–7:

> *The LORD, the LORD God, merciful and gracious, longsuffering, and abundant in goodness and truth, keeping mercy for thousands, forgiving iniquity and transgression and sin, and that will by no means clear the guilty;* ***visiting the iniquity of the fathers upon the children, and upon the children's children, unto the third and to the fourth generation.***

Although all born-again believers have ultimately been liberated from the "curse of the law" through the atoning death of Christ (see Galatians 3:13–14), we must recognize that demonic activity can still be perpetuated through bloodlines and other familiar ties. For instance, a father who commits adultery may open the door for the spirits of sexual immorality to enter into his family and affect his children, especially if that father does not repent of his sin.

Another example of generational curses that serve as a doorway to demonic activity involve oaths and fraternal orders, such as the Freemasons—a subject we will discuss in further detail under the next heading. Basically, many generational curses are perpetuated through covenants that were made by distant ancestors.

I have ministered deliverance to countless people who had experienced demonic oppression as a direct result of parental involvement in satanic activity. If you identify the source of demonic oppression as a general curse, you simply need to take authority over it, in Jesus' name, and break that curse over your life.

3. Ungodly Soul Ties

The apostle Paul admonishes us, *"Be ye not unequally yoked together with unbelievers: for what fellowship hath righteousness with unrighteousness? and what communion hath light with darkness?"* (2 Corinthians 6:14). God's Word is very clear concerning the importance of avoiding ungodly unions. As human beings, we are covenantal in nature. We were made to commune and connect with others. This communion involves not only our bodies and minds but also our souls.

Our connection with others can be a source of either godly enrichment or demonic oppression. For this reason, God says that we should be careful regarding whom and what we join ourselves with. These unions are commonly referred to as "soul ties," and they are either godly or ungodly.

An example of a godly soul tie would be the bond between fellow believers within the body of Christ. We have a telling picture of this type of soul tie in the second chapter of Colossians, where Paul prayed for a specific group of believers, *"that their hearts might be comforted, being **knit together in love**..."* (Colossians 2:2).

Another godly soul tie is the marital union of a man and a woman whose marriage is *"honourable in all, and the bed undefiled"* (Hebrews 13:4)—who are faithful to each other and whose relationship is built upon the foundation of Christ.

An ungodly soul tie is one that the Lord has not sanctioned, such as the sexual union between a woman and a man who are not married. The apostle Paul wrote about such a union in his first epistle to the Corinthians, saying, *"What? know ye not that he which is joined to an harlot is one body [with her]? for two, saith he [Jesus], shall be one flesh"* (1 Corinthians 6:16). Paul was quoting Genesis 2:24, a verse that establishes the basic guideline for a godly marriage: *"Therefore shall a man leave his father and his mother, and shall cleave unto his wife: and they shall be one flesh."*

Another ungodly soul tie, as I mentioned before, is a vow or oath made to a fraternal order or other type of secret society, such as the Freemasons, Eastern Star, or the Shriners. The term "oath" is defined by *Merriam-Webster's* as "a solemn usually formal calling upon God or a god to witness to the truth of what one says or to witness that one sincerely intends to do what one says." The definition says it all—oaths may invoke "gods" as one's witness, thereby denying the one true God. Making oaths is also known as "pledging" or "making vows."

VOWS AND OATHS GRANT PERMISSION TO DEMONIC SPIRITUAL FORCES TO OPERATE IN OUR LIVES.

Oaths can also take the form of "inner vows" made unknowingly through traumatic experiences. We see inner vows at work in the cases of women who consult "spiritual healers" to remedy barrenness or to prevent miscarriages.

In the book of Ephesians, the apostle Paul gives the following exhortation:

Have no fellowship with the unfruitful works of darkness, but rather reprove them. For it is a shame even to speak of those things which are done of them in secret. (Ephesians 5:11–12)

The word "*fellowship*" in the above passage comes from the Greek word *sugkoinōneō*, which means "to share in company with," to "be partaker of." In other words, we are commanded by God not to partake of any group that communes with darkness. Those who join themselves to ungodly fellowships, such as fraternities, sororities, and secret societies, form an ungodly soul tie and thereby open themselves to spiritual darkness.

I will grant that there are such things as "Christian fraternities," but that is not what we are discussing here. We are talking about secular fellowships, many of which blatantly reject the truth that God is the only Creator and Lord. If you or someone you know is involved with a secret society, renounce the tie immediately and declare the blood of Jesus over your mind, body, and soul.

No matter its nature, an ungodly soul tie can open the door to demonic oppression. Whenever we yoke ourselves with someone who has demonic activity operating in his or her life, we invite the same demonic activity to operate in our lives. What fellowship has light with darkness? None! And we should keep it that way in our relationships.

4. Involvement in the Occult

Occultism includes the theories, practices, and rituals based on esoteric knowledge of spirits and unknown forces. The realm of the occult includes such practices as astrology, alchemy, divination, magic, transcendental meditation, witchcraft, and sorcery.

Occultism has become widely popular in society today. Almost everywhere you look, you see the influence of these mystical practices, especially in movies, art, and music. The devil has attempted to seduce this generation into seeking another source of power and wisdom aside from God.

Any involvement in the occult, even "merely" dabbling, can immediately open the door to demonic spirits. Reading books involving witchcraft or New Age philosophy and listening to demonically influenced music are two major ways in which the occult subtly infiltrates the lives of people—believers and unbelievers alike—resulting in the propagation of fear, doubt, unbelief, and depression.

There are a large number of people in the church today who are feeling oppressed by dark forces, but many of them have no idea where these attacks are coming from. Recently, I ministered to a lady who had been battling severe spiritual attacks on her mind and emotions. She did not have the faintest idea how the devil had managed to get this kind of access to her mental and emotional life. After asking her several probing questions, I discovered that her family was deeply involved in the occult. In fact, her father had made an oath with a warlock to secure the success and prosperity of his children. As the head of the home, a father has particular spiritual authority over his children (see, for example, 1 Corinthians 11:3); and so, when a father enters into a demonic covenant with the enemy via the occult, it opens the door for spiritual oppression to affect the entire family.

As a result of the demonic oath made by this woman's father, she had been suffering from severe insomnia for months. Once we identified the open door to the devil, we took authority over the powers of darkness, in Jesus' name, and declared her freedom. The next night, the woman slept for over ten hours. Praise the name of the Lord! This is a prime example of the insidious consequences of getting involved in the occult.

Those who are involved in the occult, whether they're consulting witches and warlocks or practicing Eastern meditation, elevate these things above God—they commit idolatry. All throughout the Old Testament, we see God's disdain for the worship of idols. In the book of Deuteronomy, for example, it says, *"They provoked him to jealousy with strange gods, with abominations provoked they him to anger....And when the LORD saw it, he abhorred them..."* (Deuteronomy 32:16, 19). In fact, the first of the Ten Commandments is, *"Thou shalt have no other gods before me"* (Exodus 20:3).

It is clear that God hates idolatry. The question is, Why is God so adamant about this subject? The truth is that there are no other gods beside the one and true God, Jehovah. Idols are nothing more than demons. As the apostle Paul writes, *"The things which the Gentiles sacrifice, they sacrifice to devils, and not to God: and I would not that ye should have fellowship with devils"* (1 Corinthians 10:20). The Lord did not want the Israelites to become defiled and oppressed by demonic spirits. Satan is a counterfeiter who loves to be worshipped. It was his self-love and desire for worship that caused him to be cast out of his heavenly abode in the first place. (See Isaiah 14:12–14.)

Unfortunately, many believers violate the first commandment on a consistent basis. What is even more frightening is the fact that most of them don't even realize they are practicing idolatry. What does this have to do with overcoming the powers of darkness? We cannot overcome a kingdom that we are in agreement with. How are believers in agreement with the kingdom of darkness? It is quite simple! Countless people are involved with the New Age movement and other forms of the occult—magic, mysticism, and so forth—either knowingly or unknowingly. This involvement ranges from reading horoscopes to practicing Eastern meditation, from casting spells to consulting spiritualists or fortune-tellers.

GOD IS A JEALOUS GOD WHO WILL NOT PERMIT US TO WORSHIP HIM **AND** WORSHIP IDOLS.

Many people have become victims of demonic oppression because of their participation in the New Age movement. I have seen countless individuals in the church experience sickness, mental illness, and even poverty by entertaining New Age spirits. Many people even go as far as to justify their behavior by saying, "But I'm not hurting anyone!" The devil is a liar! God is the only true source of strength, power, healing, and wisdom, and born-again believers who seek these spiritual virtues from any other source are likely to open a doorway to the enemy.

Oftentimes, the New Age movement seems absolutely harmless, but the truth is that it is an insidious portal through which the enemy can enter a believer's life. Recently, we ministered to a woman whose child had become demonized through her mother's involvement with energy healing and acupuncture. We have also witnessed people harboring demons of New Age and other forms of false spirituality attempt to infiltrate the local church. These individuals are seen as spiritual and charismatic, due to their sensitivity to the spiritual realm, but they are not serving the Lord Jesus Christ.

Remember, the Bible says that we are not to be in fellowship with demons. (See 1 Corinthians 10:20.) A believer who realizes that he or she has had involvement in the occult should immediately repent, renounce that involvement, and take authority over any ungodly influences that he or she may have entertained, either consciously or unconsciously.

The Lord Jesus is your Deliverer, and He longs to heal and restore you today. Don't put it off any longer!

Collapsing Demonic Portals

One day, while I was driving in my car, the Holy Spirit spoke to me very clearly. He said, "Kynan! Do you see that adult film store over there?" To this question, I responded, "Yes, Lord!" Then He told me, "That store is a demonic portal for the kingdom of darkness. Through that store, spirits of addiction, rape, violence, and murder are released into the atmosphere."

Up until that point, I had never heard of a "demonic portal." Then the Lord said to me, "That portal must be closed!" All of a sudden, I felt the urge to pray like never before. In fact, every time I would pass by that establishment, I would pray in the Spirit. I would take authority over the spirits of perversion and lust that were controlling the store owner, and I would declare that the establishment must be closed, in Jesus' name.

Several months later, I drove by the building and noticed that the adult entertainment store was no longer there. It had been replaced by a tire and auto parts store. I share this story to show you that there are many places in our neighborhoods, communities, cities, and nation that are acting as demonic portals through which Satan and his demons enter and wreak havoc on unsuspecting victims.

What do I mean by the term "demonic portal"? First, let's define *portal*. A portal is a doorway, gate, or other entrance, especially a large and elaborate one. By demonic portal, we mean an open door to the enemy. As long as these doors (portals) are open, the devil will continue to operate in a specific environment or territory; but once the portal is closed, he no longer has free access to operate in that environment.

THE BLOOD OF JESUS HAS THE SUPERNATURAL POWER TO COLLAPSE DEMONIC PORTALS.

The truth is that demons are not as complex as you may think. Just like any kind of pest, they will live wherever they have the easiest access. This is why it is necessary for us to collapse every demonic portal in our lives. If you are not aware of any such portals, ask the Holy Spirit to reveal them to you.

One of the most common portals to the enemy in the lives of people is sexual immorality. Did you know that when pornography is viewed in a home, it opens a window of darkness that can oppress everyone who lives there? This is why God tells us to flee fornication. (See 1 Corinthians 6:18.) The word "pornography" is derived from the Greek word *porneia*, which refers to drawings of temple prostitutes—priestesses to the goddesses Diana and Artemis. Every time a person views pornography, he opens himself to the worship of fleshly idols that can, in turn, demonize him.

It is common for men or women with a pornography addiction to experience concurrent sickness in their bodies, lack in their finances, and even mental illness. Why? Because pornography is a gateway to even greater levels of spiritual oppression.

So, how do we collapse these portals of darkness? As we have mentioned previously, the first step is to recognize them for what they really are: evil. The second step is to repent of and renounce any activity in your life that may have opened a door to the enemy. The final step is to come under the lordship of Jesus Christ and declare that His blood has cleansed you of all sin and destroyed any and every demonic portal that had been left open in your life.

Building Altars to Jehovah

And the LORD appeared unto Abram, and said, Unto thy seed will I give this land: and there builded he an altar unto the LORD, who appeared unto him. (Genesis 12:7)

We have introduced the concept of portals from a spiritual standpoint. Again, when we use the term "portal," we are not referring to something mystical or New Age but a gateway or door through which demons have access to our lives. However, portals are not always demonic. They can also be access points to God's presence and angelic activity. You must remember that Satan is a counterfeiter. He has no originality or authenticity. Every aspect of his kingdom is a perversion of an aspect of the kingdom of God.

The concept of portals is a common biblical theme. For example, the Bible says in Genesis 28 that Jacob went to a place called Haran, where, while he slept, he had a vision of angels ascending and descending a ladder. (See Genesis 28:12.) God stood at the top of the ladder and spoke to Jacob concerning the promises He had made to Abraham. (See Genesis 28:13–15.) Jacob said to himself, *"Surely the LORD is in this place; and I knew it not.…This is none other but the house of God, and this is the **gate of heaven**"* (Genesis 28:16–17). What Jacob was actually beholding was a supernatural portal where the angels of God were descending to the earth and ascending back to heaven.

When Jacob awoke from this dream, the Bible says,

Jacob rose up early in the morning, and took the stone that he had put for his pillows, and set it up for a pillar, and poured oil upon the top of it. And he called the name of that place Bethel: but the name of that city was called Luz at the first.
(Genesis 28:18–19)

ALTARS ARE SPIRITUAL ACCESS POINTS WHERE THE REVELATION OF GOD IS PROCLAIMED AND THE WORSHIP OF GOD IS ESTABLISHED.

The word *"pillar"* comes from the Hebrew word *matstsebah*, which can refer to a monument or altar. In other words, Jacob built an altar to God in the place where he experienced this supernatural encounter. It was common during ancient times to build altars to God. Why were altars important? Because they served as divine portals through which God manifested His presence to His people. These portals (or doorways) were points of contact where heaven invaded the earth. Such was the case of the mercy seat in the tabernacle. (See Exodus 25:17.)

Although we believers of today are under the new covenant, and not the old covenant, which governed the activities of Jacob and the Israelites, the principle of altars is still relevant. Why? Altars were also used to dedicate specific territories or regions to God. They were spiritual markers, reminding God's people of His faithfulness. Altars are very important in spiritual warfare because the devil and his demons recognize them. Whatever we dedicate to God—ourselves, our finances, our time, our property, and so forth—becomes a supernatural altar, a portal of favor, blessing, and breakthrough.

In our family, we have built up "spiritual altars" where we have dedicated our family and ministry to the Lord. In the Old Testament, God commanded the Israelites to tear down the altars of Baal, an idol that represented immorality (see, for example, Judges 6:25), and to build altars to the Most High God. By building godly altars, we are telling the devil that he can't have our children, our marriage, our ministry, or anything else that belongs to the Most High. Hallelujah!

Deliverance Prayer

Heavenly Father, I thank You for breaking the power of the spirit of python over my life. Your Word declares that You have given me authority over all the power of the enemy and that nothing shall by any means hurt me. Right now, in Jesus' name, I declare that I am completely free from any and all addictions, perversions, compulsions, fears, and life-controlling issues. I loose myself from the demonic stranglehold of the spirit of python and command all depression, anxiety, and chronic sickness to leave my spirit, soul, and body, in Jesus' name. Satan, I loose myself from you and command you to leave me now! He whom the Son sets free is free indeed; therefore, I declare my complete and total freedom from this day forward, in Jesus' name.

Father, Your Word says that You are to be the only object of my worship and veneration; therefore, I declare that I will worship You alone, Lord God, and You only will I serve. I ask that You would forgive me for any form of idolatry in my life, whether known or unknown. I renounce any and all involvement with the New Age or the occult, and I command the spirits associated with them to leave my mind, body, and soul right now, in Jesus' name. I declare that the blood of Jesus collapses and destroys every demonic portal in my life and in the lives of those around me. My body is a temple of the Holy Spirit; as a result, I declare that my thoughts, meditations, words, and actions are holy and righteous. From this day forward, I will never participate in or be bound by any evil force. Thank You, Lord, for making me free and empowering me to liberate others. In Jesus' name, amen!

7

CALLED TO CONQUER

> *In all these things we are more than conquerors through him that loved us.*
> —Romans 8:37

The moment I discovered that I had authority over the devil was the moment I took a stand. No longer would I allow Satan to have his way in my life. The years of fear, bondage, and terror were over. I felt like a man being released from prison. As believers in God, we are called not only to walk in authority and freedom but also to conquer our enemy. This enemy is not physical or fleshly but spiritual.

To conquer is to overcome and take control by military force. The word conjures the image of a powerful army seizing back control of a fortress or another type of military outpost. It's time to seize control of your mind. It's time to take back control of your life. This is not a passive action; it requires spiritual force.

The Bible calls us *"more than conquerors"* (Romans 8:37). This term is derived from the Greek compound word *hupernikaō*, which means "to vanquish...gain a surpassing victory." In other words,

God doesn't want us to merely survive; He wants us to experience a surpassing victory over the enemy of our souls. And this victory is possible, because Jesus Christ has already conquered the devil! That's right, beloved; you don't have to fear. You are facing an enemy who has already been conquered.

The purpose of this book is not to convince you of how powerful the devil is; on the contrary, it is to make you realize the magnitude of God's power within you through Christ Jesus. You are powerful! You are mighty! The greater One lives and dwells the inside of you!

GOD DOES NOT WANT YOU TO COEXIST WITH THE POWERS OF DARKNESS—HE WANTS YOU TO CONQUER THEM!

Years ago, I learned about something called the exclusion principle. This principle states that two objects (or masses) cannot occupy the same space at the same time. The principle doesn't just apply to physics and chemistry; it also applies to spiritual warfare. You and the devil cannot occupy the same space at the same time. Depression and joy cannot cohabitate in the same vessel. One of them has to go! The born-again life was never intended to be occupied by fear, anxiety, and bondage. Many believers are simply trying to survive, but God did not call you to survive; He called you to reign. Once you recognize your responsibility to drive out the enemy from your life, it will change the way you view those things that are causing oppression.

In the book of Numbers, God gave the following instructions to the Israelites:

> *Then ye shall drive out all the inhabitants of the land from before you, and destroy all their pictures, and destroy all their*

> molten images, and quite pluck down all their high places: and ye shall dispossess the inhabitants of the land, and dwell therein: for I have given you the land to possess it.
>
> (Numbers 33:52–53)

In telling the Israelites to drive out all the pagan nations of people who were inhabiting the land that He was giving to them, God was also providing a type and shadow of the spiritual mandate that He would give the church—a mandate to drive out the forces of darkness.

Take It by Force!

> And from the days of John the Baptist until now the kingdom of heaven suffereth violence, and the violent take it by force.
>
> (Matthew 11:12)

We have been called to conquer the enemy's kingdom and to seize our freedom by force. Whatever demonic oppression you refuse to drive out of your life will ultimately drive you out of the path of God's blessings and promises for your life.

Growing up in the urban community, I faced my share of bullies. I can vividly remember one particular instance when I was confronted by a young man in my class who was twice my size. He would often tease me and assault me. Like any kid would, I told my father about the situation. To my surprise, I was not met with words of compassion or consolation but with this exhortation: "Defend yourself!" In my family, we were not encouraged to surrender to intimidators but instead to stand our ground.

So, per my father's instructions, I went to school the next day and faced my "enemy." I would love to say that this confrontation did not result in violence, but it did. The positive part of this story is that the young man never bullied me again. It was after this experience that I realized bullies thrive on causing intimidation and fear. Once their victim no longer appears intimidated, they lose their power. I also learned that the only way to stop a bully from tormenting you is by force.

God does not encourage us to use physical violence, but when it comes to spiritual warfare, we have to employ force to take back our freedom from Satan and his cohorts. The devil is nothing more than a bully who seeks to manipulate, intimidate, and control. His kingdom of darkness is energized by the show of fear and cowardice on the part of believers. We must realize what God has promised us, and then grab hold of those promises by force—"*violent...force.*"

THE POWERS OF DARKNESS THAT ARE OPERATING IN OUR LIVES ARE SHATTERED WHEN WE EXERT "SPIRITUAL FORCE" ACCORDING TO THE WORD OF GOD.

The word "*violence*" in Matthew 11:12 comes from the Greek word *biazō*—to use force. The word *force* is defined as "strength or energy as an attribute of physical action or movement." Simply put, force is *power in action*. Those who are willing to take action will experience God's power to bring freedom and deliverance, while those who remain passive will never experience change.

In the case of spiritual warfare, you and I must exert spiritual force in order to engage and defeat the kingdom of darkness. Too many Christians are sitting back and allowing themselves to fall victim to the enemy instead of taking action against him.

How do we take action against the enemy? The basis for all spiritual power is revelation. Once God's Word is revealed to us, and we act upon that revelation, it releases supernatural power that brings freedom and deliverance in our lives. We also exert spiritual force through the spoken Word of God. If the enemy is oppressing you, don't remain silent; open your mouth and declare God's Word. Remember, *"they overcame him [Satan] by…the word of their testimony"* (Revelation 12:11). By consistently speaking God's Word, you are releasing spiritual breakthrough. It is only a matter of time before the devil will have to back off.

Nothing in your life will change until you take action, and you will never take action until you have received revelation. Revelation from God's Word has the power to move us from where we are to where He intends for us to be.

The Anointing Destroys the Yoke

And it shall come to pass in that day, that his burden shall be taken away from off thy shoulder, and his yoke from off thy neck, and the yoke shall be destroyed because of the anointing. (Isaiah 10:27)

In the gospel of Luke, chapter 4, Jesus went into the synagogue in Nazareth on the Sabbath and stood up to read from the scroll. He opened to the book of Isaiah and read:

The Spirit of the Lord is upon me, because he hath anointed me to preach the gospel to the poor; he hath sent me to heal the brokenhearted, to preach deliverance to the captives, and recovering of sight to the blind, to set at liberty them that are bruised…. (Luke 4:18)

This verse of Scripture echoes Isaiah 61:1 and masterfully illustrates the power of the anointing of the Holy Spirit. We will not succeed in taking dominion over the kingdom of darkness without a proper understanding of the anointing.

What is "the anointing"? The word "anointing" comes from the Greek word *chriō*, which means "to smear or rub with ointment." In the Old Testament, the anointing (*shemen*, in Hebrew) is expressed as oil or ointment. This medicinal oil, or anointing, represents the power and presence of the Holy Spirit working in and through us. Jesus was the Anointed One (*Christos*) sent by God to liberate God's people. Through the anointing, Jesus Christ manifested the kingdom of God on the earth.

THE ANOINTING OF THE HOLY SPIRIT DESTROYS EVERY YOKE OF BONDAGE AND RELEASES PEOPLE FROM CAPTIVITY.

Simply put, the anointing is the miracle-working, burden-removing, yoke-destroying power of God. A supernatural power that's released through the Holy Spirit, the anointing frees the people of God from life-controlling issues, bondages, and oppression.

The Bible says, "*The anointing which ye have received of him abideth in you*" (1 John 2:27). This is amazing! The same anointing that was upon Jesus Christ—the anointing that set the captives free—lives and dwells on the inside of you! This means that there is no bondage in your life that's more powerful than the supernatural anointing resident in your inner being. So, what are you waiting for? If the anointing already abides in you, then why are you allowing Satan to torment you? You already have the supernatural equipment that you need in order to deal with the devil. All you have to do is release it!

Did you know that there is enough of the Holy Spirit inside of you to set you free? Romans 8:11 assures us, "*If the Spirit of him that raised up Jesus from the dead dwell in you, he that raised up Christ from the dead shall also quicken your mortal bodies by his Spirit that dwelleth in you.*" The moment you realize that the same Spirit that raised Jesus from the dead dwells in you, the power of addiction, bondage, sickness, fear, anxiety, and depression will be broken, once and for all.

You may be asking, "If I am so anointed, then why do I feel so defeated?" Jesus recognized and acknowledged the anointing that the Father placed upon Him before He was able to walk in the power of God. We must do the same thing. An anointing you fail to recognize is an anointing you fail to release. But once you place a demand on the anointing by faith, the supernatural breakthrough, freedom, and deliverance that you need will manifest, in Jesus' name.

We Are Kings and Priests

Were you aware that, from a spiritual standpoint, you and I are kings and priests?

> *Jesus Christ…is the faithful witness, and the first begotten of the dead, and the prince of the kings of the earth. Unto him that loved us, and washed us from our sins in his own blood, and hath made us kings and priests unto God and his Father; to him be glory and dominion forever and ever. Amen.*
> (Revelation 1:5–6)

Our understanding of the mantle of king and priest is of paramount importance in our ability to live a victorious life. Earlier, we discussed the necessity of exerting spiritual force and releasing the anointing in order to conquer the powers of darkness. Now we will take a deeper look at the role and responsibility of every believer to advance the kingdom of God as a king and a priest.

The word "king" comes from the Greek word *basileus*, which refers to a leader of the people, prince, commander, or lord of the land. What is the role of a king? It is the king's responsibility to rule and to reign. Ontologically speaking, every born-again, blood-washed believer has been called to exercise rule and authority in the spiritual realm. We are not God, but we are His children, and as such, we have been commissioned as vice-regents in the rule of His kingdom.

When was the last time that you saw a king begging on the side of the road? That would be unheard of! Yet there are so many believers in Jesus who are living well beneath the level of their inheritance in Christ. Religion and tradition teach us that we don't have any power in this life, but nothing could be further from the truth. Beloved, you have been given authority to rule and reign in the earth.

GOD HAS GIVEN US, AS KINGS, SPIRITUAL RULE OVER ALL THE POWERS OF DARKNESS.

We know from the testimony of Scripture that every believer has been ordained a king, but it doesn't end there. Along with kingship and rule, God has placed upon us the mantle of priest. What is a priest? It is one who offers sacrifices on behalf of others. In the Old Testament, the role of the priest was to make intercession to God on behalf of the people and to offer blood sacrifices to cover their sins. The priests served as mediators between God and man.

With the New Testament, the priesthood was done away with when Jesus Christ became our High Priest through His atoning sacrifice on the cross. (See, for example, Hebrews 6:20.) As a result, we no longer need a human mediator to pray to God or make sacrifices on our behalf, because Jesus Christ is our Mediator; He *"is even at the right hand of God, who also maketh intercession for us"* (Romans 8:34).

Even so, we have been called by God to intercede for others through the ministry of reconciliation, whereby we have the divine right and supernatural endowment to make intercession for people, communities, and nations. This is absolutely wonderful! As kings and priests, we are charged with advancing God's kingdom in the earth and reconciling communities back to God through prayer and intercession. Everywhere we go becomes God's province and temple. This is why the devil wages war against the saints—because we play a vital role in bringing God's redemptive purposes to pass in these last days.

As a king, you can make decrees, and they will be established. As a priest, you can pray to the Father in Jesus' name, and whatever you ask for shall surely come to pass. Glory to God! Now that you know your identity as a king and a priest, you can exercise authority and rule over the devil.

Taking Back Territory

When my wife and I were newly married, we moved into our first home. We were so excited to be married that we somehow overlooked the fact that this house was located in an extremely undesirable neighborhood, to say the least. The day we moved our furniture into the home, a drug addict stole our antique piano. I have no idea how he accomplished this feat, as the piano weighed four hundred pounds!

Suffice it to say that the neighborhood was rough. By night, prostitution, drug dealing, and violence raged around our home. In fact, the residence directly across from ours was known for being a crack house that doubled as a headquarters for prostitution.

To be honest with you, I didn't pay much attention to our environment because I assumed it was just a situation we would have to accept as long as we lived in this community. I had bought the devil's lie!

One day, my mother-in-law (I call her my "mother-in-love") came to visit us, and everything changed. She sat us down and began questioning us about "the house across the street." As someone who worked in the legal field, her senses were attuned to the point that she had noticed the serious illegal activities transpiring around that house. When she asked me, "What are you going to do about it?" my first thought was, *Nothing. What can I do?* Then my mother-in-love said the strangest thing I had ever heard: "You can pray them out of this neighborhood." All of a sudden, it dawned on me that because the Bible calls us kings and priests, God has given us authority over *all* the power of the enemy—including drugs, prostitution, and violence.

So, we prayed! And would you believe, a few weeks later, those drug dealers, pimps, and prostitutes were gone? The house mysteriously closed down without any physical intervention on our part.

IT IS TIME FOR THE BODY OF CHRIST TO TAKE BACK ALL TERRITORY THAT BELONGS TO GOD—IN OTHER WORDS, ALL TERRITORY!

When Joshua assumed Moses' position as the leader of God's people, God said to him, *"Every place that the sole of your foot shall tread upon, that have I given unto you, as I said unto Moses"* (Joshua 1:3). This territory was the same land that had been promised to Abraham, Isaac, and Jacob. And while this promise referred to physical land intended for the descendants of Abraham, it applies to the church today in a spiritual sense. Everywhere the soles of our feet tread is God's property.

The word *territory* is defined as "an area of land under the jurisdiction of a ruler or state." The territory of God includes our homes, neighborhoods, schools, churches, and cities. Just as my wife and I, through prayer, took back our block from the devil, God wants you to reclaim your home, your family, and your marriage, in Jesus' name. No longer will the devil oppress your children, spread violence in your community, or release perversion in your city when you take back the territory that belongs to God!

We will not accomplish this by marching on the capital or debating in the halls of Congress but by exercising our spiritual authority. We can enter into our prayer closets as priests of the Most High and implore the power of the Holy Spirit to bring about the transformation of our cities. We can cast down principalities of darkness that are ruling over specific geographic territories and declare those places "holy ground." Wherever we refuse to advance God's kingdom, we are giving the devil permission to occupy.

After receiving his marching orders from God, Joshua said to the people of Israel,

> *Hereby ye shall know that the living God is among you, and that he will without fail drive out from before you the Canaanites, and the Hittites, and the Hivites, and the Perizzites, and the Girgashites, and the Amorites, and the Jebusites....*
>
> (Joshua 3:10)

God wants us to drive out the "Canaanites, Hittites, Hivites, Perizzites, Girgashites, Amorites, and Jebusites"—anything that stands in the way of His kingdom's advancement—and possess the land that He has promised to give us. These demonic forces have no intention of leaving, but we can force them out by the power of the Holy Spirit.

Deliverance Prayer

Father, in the name of Jesus Christ, I thank You for who You are and for all that You have done. Today, I declare that I am a king and a priest unto God, through the blood of the Lamb of God, Jesus Christ. Right now, I decree that any and all territory taken from me or from my bloodlines by the wicked one must be returned to me, in Jesus' name.

I command Satan and all his demons to loose their stranglehold on my mind, emotions, health, finances, ministry, family, career, and community. Today is the day of my supernatural breakthrough. I decree and declare, according to Isaiah 10:27, that every yoke of the devil is destroyed because of the anointing. I walk in the supernatural power and purpose of God for my life. The kingdom of darkness is demolished, disintegrated, and destroyed by the power of the Holy Spirit flowing in and through my spirit. I declare that Satan and his demons are terrified by my presence because I carry the kingdom of God in my inner being. Thank You, Lord, for my total freedom and deliverance, in Jesus' name. Amen!

DRESSED FOR BATTLE

Put on the whole armor of God, that ye may be able to stand against the wiles of the devil.
—Ephesians 6:11

So far, we have highlighted the importance of understanding true authority, knowing who we are in Christ, identifying the devil's strategies, and exposing demonic activity. Seeing that we are already engaged in spiritual warfare, whether we like it or not, it is absolutely critical that we know how to dress for the battle.

Every soldier is outfitted with a uniform and weapons for the purposes of self-defense and offensive action against the enemy. The apostle Paul had this in mind when he urged us in Ephesians 6 to put on the *"whole armor of God."* The phrase *"whole armor"* comes from the Greek word *panoplia*, which literally means "full armor"—the complete set.

In the physical sense, a full set of armor, at least in Paul's day, would have included a shield, a sword, a lance, a helmet, a pair of greaves (armor protecting the shins), and a breastplate. Paul used each of these items to illustrate a specific aspect of what we must wear in order to be fully and completely dressed for spiritual battle. To go to war without a full set of armor is to expose oneself to physical hazard and possible death. In the same manner, to neglect any aspect of our "spiritual armor" is to open ourselves up to the onslaught of the kingdom of darkness.

What is the purpose of this spiritual armor? Paul makes it very clear: *"to stand against the wiles of the devil"* (Ephesians 6:11). The word *"stand,"* from the Greek word *histēmi*, means make firm, fixed, established; be kept intact; stand unharmed. In other words, God wants us to stand our ground! He wants us to remain undaunted by the adversary.

GOD HAS PREPARED SUPERNATURAL ARMOR FOR YOU AND ME TO WEAR THAT WILL ENSURE LASTING VICTORY OVER THE ENEMY.

What are we standing against? We are standing against the "wiles," or cunning tactics, of the enemy—the deceitful artifices and trickery he employs in an effort to penetrate your spiritual defenses and take you out of the will and purposes of God. Too many believers are ignorant of the enemy's strategies, and others are improperly dressed for battle.

I have learned throughout the years that the tactics of the devil do not change, and neither does the need for our armor. The phrase *"put on,"* as used in Ephesians 6:11, comes from the Greek word *enduō*, which signifies "sinking into a garment" and clothing oneself. The idea is that we are to "sink into" this armor permanently, never to take it off as long as we live on this earth and are subject to Satan's schemes. Unlike natural armor, spiritual armor must remain on at all times! I have heard various believers say, "I had to put my armor on today." This is not a biblical concept, because the devil will not wait for you to get dressed before he attacks you. What about when you're sleeping? You are essentially defenseless, aside from whatever spiritual armor you have on. So, we must put on our armor and keep it on!

Remember, Satan is an experienced military strategist who loves taking advantage of spiritual negligence on the part of believers. If he can convince you that spiritual warfare is optional, he has already gotten you to yield to his deception. We must make a stand! We must be prepared for battle. The Word of God tells us exactly how to defeat the enemy! Let's get dressed in our armor—for good.

The Components of Our Armor

In the sixth chapter of Ephesians, the apostle Paul lists the seven components of our spiritual armor. The number seven is significant, in that it signifies completion and/or perfection. In other words, the full armor of God perfectly addresses every aspect of spiritual warfare.

There are two dimensions to any legitimate military strategy: offense and defense. Every soldier must be adequately equipped to engage in an offensive attack on the enemy. However, if a soldier is equipped only for offense, and does not have the proper tools to defend himself, then he is destined for failure. For this cause, God has given us weapons and armor that are both offensive and defensive, that we might succeed in spiritual battle.

The armor of spiritual warfare includes the following:

1. The Girdle of Truth

Ephesians 6:14 says, *"Stand therefore, having your loins girt about with truth...."* What was Paul referring to? As a brilliant scholar and teacher, he knew how to relate commonly known information with profound spiritual truths. Ephesus was a Roman province in Asia Minor, so the people in this community were well acquainted with the military armor of Roman legionaries. The loin girdle was a very basic yet important component to the Roman soldier's outfit. Why? Because it was the belt to which every weapon was fastened. In other words, Paul was telling us that before we can fight the enemy, we must be established on and fastened to the truth.

The second purpose of the loin girdle was to strengthen the core of the soldier. It was similar to a weight belt, which would have been used to provide additional support to a soldier, that he might endure the weight of his heavy armor.

In a spiritual sense, we as believers must be equipped with the knowledge of the truth. The enemy is buffeting many believers because they are ignorant of God's truth or may even be walking in deception. An ignorant believer is a spiritually weak believer! The word *truth* also implies "freedom from pretense," which means that spiritual authenticity is very important when it comes to spiritual warfare. We must walk in the truth—truly!

2. The Breastplate of Righteousness

Ephesians 6:14 goes on to say that we should "[have] *on the breastplate of righteousness.*" A breastplate was of utmost importance to the soldiers of Paul's day because it guarded the vital organs of its wearer. Without a breastplate, soldiers would be vulnerable to stabs and other forms of physical trauma.

The word "*righteousness*" comes from the Greek word *dikaiosunē*, which refers to right standing before, or a condition acceptable to, God. The concept of righteousness implies both right positioning in relation to God and right living in relation to moral purity and correctness. When we have accepted Christ's righteousness as our breastplate, then we are in a position of confidence that enables us to stand firm against the enemy.

Unrighteousness, on the other hand, produces fear and insecurity; but the unsullied confidence that comes from Christ's righteousness protects us—especially our hearts—from the attacks of Satan.

The average Christian does not fully understand righteousness. More than mere moral living, righteousness is the ability to think, to be, and to act in a way that reflects your true identity—God's perspective of who you are. When you realize that you are the righteousness of God in Christ Jesus (see 2 Corinthians 5:21), then guilt, shame, and condemnation will lose their power. The revelation of God's righteousness in you will neutralize the vicious spiritual attacks on your soul.

3. The Preparation of the Gospel of Peace

Ephesians 6:15 exhorts us, "[Have] *your feet shod with the preparation of the gospel of peace.*" What does this mean? Let's begin with "*shod*"—"furnished or equipped with a shoe," according to *Merriam-Webster's*. Simply put, the Bible is referring to shoes—sandals, specifically, as would have been worn by Roman soldiers in Paul's day. Without sandals, we cannot endure the harsh terrain of battle.

In other words, we must be prepared to share and proclaim the gospel at all times, wherever our shod feet may take us. Spiritual readiness is an essential part of spiritual warfare. Many saints are suffering from spiritual oppression because they are immobile and stagnant. They don't consistently share their faith with others, and, as a result, they are unprepared to engage the enemy on the terrain of spiritual battle.

The more you study and meditate on the Word of God with a desire to minister to others, the more victories you will see in your life. If you want to break out of depression, minister God's Word to an unbeliever. Go to the highways and byways and share the good news of Jesus, and watch your situation turn around. Don't wait until you're in the heat of the battle to try locating a Scripture to quote—be ready at all times!

4. The Shield of Faith

Paul says in Ephesians 6:16, *"Above all, [take] the shield of faith, wherewith ye shall be able to quench all the fiery darts of the wicked."* Faith is just about the most important thing in the Christian life. In fact, the Bible says that without faith, we will find it impossible to please God. (See Hebrews 11:6.)

What does faith have to do with spiritual warfare? The answer is, Everything! We will discuss the importance of taking the shield of faith in a later chapter, but for now, I want to highlight the supernatural power that faith has to neutralize demonic attacks. Notice that the Scripture says, *"Above all...."* This is not a filler word but rather a phrase used intentionally to express the preeminence of faith in spiritual warfare.

Without a shield, the most experienced soldier would be dead in seconds in a real combat situation. In the same manner, without faith in God's Word, you and I will not be able to withstand the *"fiery darts"* of the devil.

In Paul's day, combatants would throw literal flaming javelins at the enemy, designed to penetrate the defenses of the opposing army. For this reason, the Romans would soak their leather shields in water, in order to extinguish any darts that might strike them.

Faith is the shield of the spiritual realm. Through our confidence in God, we are able to extinguish every lie of the devil. In other words, the more we place our faith and trust in God, the less effective the enemy's tactics will be against us.

5. The Helmet of Salvation

Ephesians 6:17 says, *"Take the helmet of salvation...."* The verb *dechomai* is used for *"take,"* meaning that we must exert effort when it comes to gaining assurance of our salvation. Why is it called the "helmet of salvation"? The reason we must "wear" salvation, or deliverance, as a helmet is because the mind is the seat of all spiritual battle. If we don't renew our mind with the Word of God, then we will not be able to walk in victory.

Salvation doesn't just mean the deliverance of our soul from hell; it also means the deliverance of our mind from wrong thoughts and attitudes. Wrong thoughts, if left unaddressed, have the potential to enslave us. This is why the Bible says that we must take the helmet of salvation—to guard our mind and our thought life against the lies, deceptions, and accusations of the enemy.

The enemy of our soul is always trying to convince us that we are not saved. He accuses us before the Father night and day. (See Revelation 12:10.) Whenever we sin or fall short, the devil is standing by, telling us that we are not children of God. He says, "You don't love God; if you did, you wouldn't have argued with your spouse." In these times, it is important for us to acknowledge the helmet of salvation. We must take every wrong thought captive, in the name of Jesus, and continually remind ourselves, "I am a child of God through the blood of Jesus, and my sins and transgressions have been forgiven." Oftentimes, believers are not aware that the negative thoughts that come into their mind have been "sown" by the wicked one. The helmet of salvation empowers the believer to take control of the mind and to bring every ungodly thought into captivity.

6. The Sword of the Spirit

Ephesians 6:17 instructs us to *"take...the sword of the Spirit, which is the word of God."* Up until this point, every single article of spiritual armor that we have identified has been a defensive weapon. Now we're taking an offensive stance. The word *"sword"* comes from the Greek word *machaira*, which refers to a large knife, used for killing animals and cutting up flesh. This is the only offensive weapon listed by Paul in Ephesians 6. In other words, the sword of the Spirit—the Word of God—is our primary weapon for attacking the enemy.

We talked earlier about how Jesus "fought" (resisted) the devil with the Word of God in the Judean wilderness. (See Matthew 4:1–11; Luke 4:1–13.) He also fought using the Word in the garden of Gethsemane: When the soldiers dispatched by the chief priests came to arrest Him, and one of the disciples cut off the ear of a servant of the high priest, Jesus told him to put away his sword, saying, *"Thinkest thou that I cannot now pray to my Father, and he shall presently give me more than twelve legions of angels? But how then shall the scriptures be fulfilled, that thus it must be?"* (Matthew 26:53–54). And He fought with the Word on the cross, at one point crying out, *"Father, into thy hands I commend my spirit"* (Luke 23:46), which echoed the Old Testament Scripture *"Into thine hand I commit my spirit: thou hast redeemed me, O Lord God of truth"* (Psalm 31:5).

The Word of God is the source of the life-giving power of God, without which you will never be able to overcome the onslaughts of the devil. Just like a sword or knife used in physical battle, the Word of God is our greatest weapon in spiritual battle. The author of Hebrews even likened it to a sword with this statement: *"The word of God is quick, and powerful, and sharper than any twoedged sword"* (Hebrews 4:12).

You must keep in mind that Satan knows the Word of God—he is well aware of the power it contains. When the enemy comes against your health, your mind, your money, your ministry, or another area of your life, you can declare the Word of the living God.

The *"word"* of God referenced in Ephesians 6:17 is taken from the Greek word *rhema*, which means that which is uttered by the living voice. Thus, it is not enough to simply memorize a bunch of Bible verses; we must also receive revelation from the Word of God and speak forth that revelatory word in order to release the power of God for freedom, deliverance, and change. Once we have received revelation, the Word of God becomes a sword in our mouths that wreaks destruction to the kingdom of darkness. You must speak the Word (capitalized—the Bible) and the word (revelation)!

7. The Mantle of Intercession

Paul concludes his catalog of spiritual armor with the following charge: "[Pray] *always with all prayer and supplication in the Spirit, and* [watch] *thereunto with all perseverance and supplication for all saints*" (Ephesians 6:18). Contrary to popular belief, prayer is not simply a means to get what we want from God; it is also a vital weapon in spiritual warfare. Prayer is not something we do after we have put on the armor of God; it is a vital component of the entire process, starting before we even clothe ourselves in the armor and lasting long after we are properly attired for battle. Without prayer, no other portion of God's armor will operate properly in your life.

Unfortunately, prayer is one of the most neglected aspects of Christian living, even though God has stated very clearly, *"Mine house shall be called an house of prayer for all people"* (Isaiah 56:7). In other words, we have been called by God to make intercession in the earth.

Paul was talking specifically about praying in the Spirit, which is, in fact, the only possible way to fulfill his charge to *"pray without ceasing"* (1 Thessalonians 5:17). Praying in the Spirit guarantees that our prayers are heard and understood—even when we don't entirely understand what we ought to be praying for! As Paul tells us in Romans 8:26, *"The Spirit also helpeth our infirmities: for we know not what we should pray for as we ought: but the Spirit itself maketh intercession for us with groanings which cannot be uttered."*

Every time we pray in the Holy Spirit, we are building our spiritual man and equipping ourselves for spiritual battle. Whether you can see or perceive the battle ahead is irrelevant; the Holy Spirit, being omniscient, knows every scheme, plot, and strategy of the wicked one before it ever materializes. *"Praying always"* (Ephesians 6:18) implies a fixed position or posture of prayer. It is not just something we do in emergency situations. Rather, we are called by God to continually live a lifestyle of prayer and intercession, and to expect that what we have asked for will manifest. (See, for example, Matthew 21:22.)

The devil hates prayer! That is why he wars against the mind of the believer—to keep us out of our prayer chamber. He knows that every time we pray to the Father in Jesus' name, through the Holy Ghost, we wreak havoc on his plans.

Deliverance Prayer

Father, in Jesus' name, I thank You for Your goodness and grace operating in my life. I thank You, Lord, that You have granted me the supernatural armor necessary to both defend myself against the enemy and tear down his counterfeit kingdom. I hereby take up the breastplate of righteousness and the helmet of salvation, which guard my heart, mind, and soul against guilt, shame, and condemnation and grant me the holy boldness to engage the enemy on the battlefield of my mind.

I decree that every assault of the enemy is thwarted, in Jesus' name. I declare that I am victorious over the enemy and that no weapon formed against me shall prosper. I cast down all thoughts of fear, doubt, and unbelief right now, in Jesus' name. I know in my heart that the devil is the father of lies; therefore, I declare that my loins are girt with the truth of God's Word. No attack of the enemy will prevail against me again, in Jesus' name. Amen!

TAKING DOMINION

> *God said, Let us make man in our image, after our likeness: and let them have dominion over the fish of the sea, and over the fowl of the air, and over the cattle, and over all the earth, and over every creeping thing that creepeth upon the earth.*
> —Genesis 1:26

Of all that we have discussed so far, the most important truth to understand is God's original design for creating mankind and placing him in the earthly realm. We were created and called to take dominion on the earth. Why is this important to remember when discussing spiritual warfare? Jesus told us that we have power (authority) over the enemy. (See, for example, Luke 10:19.) If you don't recognize and accept God's plan for you to take dominion over the earth, then you won't recognize that the devil and all his demons are subject to you as a child of God.

What does the term "dominion" really mean? It comes from the Hebrew word *radah*, which means "to…tread down, i.e. subjugate;…to reign,…rule (over)." In other words, humankind was given the divine right to bring everything in the earth under subjugation to the government and authority of God's kingdom. Man was literally commissioned to colonize the earth, and in such a way that it would come to resemble heaven. That is the reason we were told to pray, "*Thy kingdom come. Thy will be done in earth, as it is in heaven*" (Matthew 6:10).

That is also exactly what Jesus did during His earthly ministry—He brought the kingdom to the earth! And if we are born-again believers in Jesus Christ, we have been called to do as He did. (See John 14:12.) The pattern of the garden of Eden was a prophetic symbol of the church. Just as Adam had the spiritual authority to tread on, or have dominion over, everything in the garden, we have the right to tread on the powers of darkness. In fact, the word *radah* can also mean "to scrape out." Scraping involves pushing or pulling a sharp implement across a surface so as to remove dirt or some other matter. In other words, you and I have been called to remove the residue of Satan's kingdom from every area of our lives, even throughout the earth!

GOD HAS CALLED THE CHURCH TO EXTEND HIS KINGDOM THROUGHOUT THE WHOLE EARTH.

The idea of dominion is much greater than you might realize. Many of us know that God has given us authority over the devil, according to Luke 10:19, but we may be ignorant of our responsibility to take dominion. Authority and dominion are not the same. Authority is simply the legal right to act in a certain way, while dominion is the consequential action we undertake.

Once a king is crowned, he gains the legal right to rule, but he still needs to take dominion in order for his kingdom to be established. Dominion, then, is the active rule and supremacy God has granted us to exercise so that His kingdom will be established in reality. Our heavenly Father is not interested merely in our salvation; He also wants us to function as His vice-regents in the earth, literally ruling over the powers of darkness.

When we understand our right and responsibility to take dominion, our presence alone will cause demons to tremble. Remember, through Jesus Christ, we have been anointed and ordained as kings and priests. Our kingship extends beyond the four walls of the church and permeates every area of our lives, from our families to our communities to our careers. No matter what the devil has done, you have dominion over him—you just need to exercise it.

The Kingdom of God Is All-powerful

We have already discussed Revelation 1:6, which says that God *"hath made us kings and priests unto God and his Father"* (Revelation 1:6). What are the implications of our kingship? As kings, we have been given the right and the power to rule and reign in the earthly realm. This is a spiritual kingship, which means that anything operating on the earth falls under our spiritual jurisdiction. Whether it be sickness, disease, oppression, fear, or any other demonic force, it has been subjected to our spiritual authority.

When a king makes a decree, it becomes established as law throughout his kingdom. This is what Jesus meant when He said,

> *I will give unto thee the keys of the kingdom of heaven: and whatsoever thou shalt bind on earth shall be bound in heaven: and whatsoever thou shalt loose on earth shall be loosed in heaven.* (Matthew 16:19)

According to our Lord Jesus, whatever we declare to be lawful and correct in the earth is deemed lawful in heaven, and whatever we deem to be unlawful and unacceptable in earth is likewise unlawful and unacceptable in heaven. Do you realize how much power and authority you have? Do you understand the sovereign power of God's kingdom?

GOD'S KINGDOM IS PREEMINENT OVER ANY OTHER KINGDOM IN EXISTENCE.

For over 1,600 years, the church has misunderstood the concept of the sovereignty of God. We have painted God as some cruel deity who does whatever He wants to whomever He chooses. Some people have even gone so far as to say that God is the one responsible for sickness and calamity in the world today. Nothing could be further from the truth! God's sovereignty is expressed through us, His children, the church of the Lord Jesus Christ. We are His spiritual representatives on the earth.

God governs His kingdom through His sovereign Word. Whatever He has declared in His Word is the standard by which He governs the entire kingdom. When we understand sovereignty from this vantage point, it will transform our lives, because we will realize that God has granted the church sovereign power over the devil. As a result, we have the ability to break generational curses in our family lines and declare that they will never operate again. We have the power to curse terminal illness and command it to cease and desist, in Jesus' name.

The devil has attempted, through religion and tradition, to talk the church out of its power. Many people have abdicated their authority by sitting back and waiting for God to do what He has granted them the authority to do. Things don't "just happen," beloved! The only way you will experience lasting change and victory in your life is by walking in the spiritual power and authority your heavenly Father has already given you. Now is the time to take dominion. Now is the time to draw a line in the sand.

God's Kingdom Is More than Words

The questions remain: If we are a part of this all-powerful kingdom of God, then why do we still experience bondage and defeat in our lives? Why does the devil still attack and persecute us? Many people know what the Bible says, yet they continue to be oppressed by fear and despondency. What is the reason for this disconnect?

The apostle Paul tells us, *"For the kingdom of God is not in word, but in power"* (1 Corinthians 4:20). To put it another way, the kingdom of God does not consist of mere talk or moral precepts but of the demonstration of God's limitless power. Many people talk about God, but they are not experiencing His power to change their lives. This power that Paul is referring to is the *dunamis* power of God. *Dunamis* is a Greek term that means "miraculous power," or the power resident in a thing by virtue of its nature. Simply put, the kingdom of God must be demonstrated in every area of our life, to such a degree that we experience change and lasting transformation.

Some people are being taught philosophy and theology, but they have never experienced this *dunamis* power. Like any madman, the devil will not respond to reason, logic, or theology; he responds only to power.

Imagine a terrorist trying to break into the Pentagon. He is not coming to talk or negotiate; he is bent on murder and destruction. The only way to address this assailant is to demonstrate your power. In the same manner, it is time for believers to stop talking and start demonstrating the power of God. How do we release this power? The power of God's kingdom is released through revelation.

REVELATION IS THE KEY TO EXPERIENCING THE POWER OF GOD IN EVERY AREA OF LIFE.

In these last days, it is absolutely necessary that our local churches become what Jesus intended them to be. It is critical for us, as the body of Christ, to be a community that demonstrates the love and power of God and does not merely talk about it in a thirty-minute sermon every Sunday. People should be able to come to the house of God and be healed and delivered. The biggest indictment against the church of the Lord Jesus is not that we lack perfection or have too much sin but that we have failed to make a spiritual impact on our generation. Wherever a church exists, the community surrounding it should be permanently altered by the church's presence there. The children should be transformed because their parents serve the true and living God.

It is time for us to stop simply quoting Bible verses and to start living out what the Bible promises. The devil is afraid of us because he knows our supernatural potential. The question is, Do you know what—or Who—lives in you? This is the reason why so many believers are still bound: They have yet to realize or experience the sovereign power of God.

The day I realized that God's kingdom is more than mere words, everything in my life took a dramatic turn. From that moment on, when I spoke, things happened. When I prayed, I received divine answers. When I laid hands on the sick, they recovered. The key is recognizing that the kingdom of God is on the inside of you, and that it is more powerful than the kingdom of darkness.

We don't have to be victims of fear and oppression any longer. We are ambassadors of the Lord Jesus, endued with His strength, power, and ability. Once you have a revelation of who Jesus is—and who He is in *you*—the powers of darkness will never prevail against you again!

The Kingdom of God Is Within You

We stated previously that the kingdom of God is an omnipotent kingdom, because God is almighty. This means that there are no limits to His power. Have you taken time to ponder the ramifications of this truth? Again, the Bible says, *"Behold, the kingdom of God is **within you**"* (Luke 17:21). What did Jesus mean when

He said that the kingdom of God was within us? As you know by now, the kingdom of God is the government of God in heaven and on earth; therefore, He meant that we carry the government and dominion of God on the inside of us. This means that wherever we go, the kingdom of God goes with us.

Jesus modeled this paradigm during His earthly ministry. He said, *"If I cast out devils by the Spirit of God, then the kingdom of God is come unto you"* (Matthew 12:28). Every supernatural miracle Jesus performed, every demon He cast out, was a manifestation of God's kingdom on the earth. It was through the power of His kingdom that He was able to release people from captivity to demonic spirits and destructive habits. In the same manner, the power of the kingdom releases us from any and all evil bondage.

The good news is that we don't have to wait for Jesus to return to earth and touch us, because He has already manifested His power on the inside of us. This is the power, dominion, and rule of God that affects every area of our lives. The more conscious you are of the dominion of God inside your soul, the more it will grow and expand, reaching out to affect the world around you.

GOD HAS CALLED AND EQUIPPED US TO RELEASE THE KINGDOM OF GOD FROM WITHIN!

If the kingdom of God is on the inside of you, how do you get it out? You must release the kingdom! But you can't release something you don't know you have. Many people are waiting on God to deal with the devil in their lives. Meanwhile, Satan torments, afflicts, and buffets them until they cave in to his manipulation. This is not God's will! You already have the tools that you need to defeat the enemy. You are a carrier of the sovereign government of God. The devil wants you to believe that you are nothing more than a spectator or a "pew-warmer," but the truth is that you are fully equipped and fully furnished to take dominion.

Fifteen years ago, I did not know the truths that I am sharing with you today. I thought that the devil was stronger than I. He preyed on my fear and kept me intimidated of him. But now I have dedicated my entire existence to advancing God's kingdom in every sphere of society.

The Bible says, "*God anointed Jesus of Nazareth with the Holy Ghost and with power: who went about doing good, and healing all that were oppressed of the devil; for God was with him*" (Acts 10:38). Jesus knew that there was no coexisting with the kingdom of darkness; the only option was to drive out the enemy. And God has called you and me to do the same! He wants you to be free so that you can liberate other people and bring them to a place of healing and wholeness. Did you know that God has chosen you to be a deliverer of your generation? There is no cavalry coming; you are it! Just remember, greater is He who lives in you than he who lives in the world. (See 1 John 4:4.) This revelation shifted my life, and it will shift your life, as well.

The Gates of Hell Will Not Prevail

Growing up in a Christian home, I never gave much thought or consideration to attending church. It was just something we were required to do; otherwise, we were disciplined by my mother. In fact, I regret to say that I despised church. I viewed it as a building full of religious posers who sang songs, gave offerings, and talked about things they didn't really believe.

It wasn't until I came to faith in Christ and started reading the Bible for myself that I realized the church was far from what I had long assumed. My religious concept of church was totally wrong!

What is the church? Jesus told Peter in Matthew 16:18, "*Upon this rock I will build my church; and the gates of hell shall not prevail against it.*" Here, Jesus used the Greek word *ekklēsia* to designate the church. *Ekklēsia* is a compound word, made up of the preposition *ek*, which means "out among" or "from," and the verb *kaleo*, "to call (forth)." A political expression, it denotes a gathering of citizens who have been "called out" from their homes to a public assembly. In other words, the church is the legislative body of saints, called out of the world system to convene in a spiritual assembly as representatives of the kingdom of God on earth.

When was the last time you thought of the church in this manner? Very few in the body of Christ realize the spiritual significance and magnitude of the church's high calling. The church is meant to be far more than worship services, coffee shops, and youth ministry. God has placed the church on the earth to legislate the matters of His kingdom in the earthly realm. The church is the only barrier between Satan and society!

THE CHURCH IS A SUPERNATURAL COMMUNITY MADE UP OF BELIEVERS ENDOWED WITH SPIRITUAL POWER AND AUTHORITY.

Now that you have a deeper understanding of the church and its purpose, you can grasp the second part of what Jesus said in Matthew 16:18: *"...and the gates of hell shall not prevail against it."* The word *"gates"* comes from the Greek word *pulē* and may have indicated the wall surrounding a palace, temple, or fortress—thus, the seat of political power and authority for the kingdom of darkness. The Bible says that the church will be built upon the revelation of Jesus Christ. What is the revelation of Jesus? He is both Lord and King! Once we have the revelation of who He is and who we are, the thrones, authorities, and influences of hell will not be able to prevail, overtake, overcome, or exert their power over the church of the Lord Jesus.

The word *"prevail"* implies being superior in strength. In other words, once we, the church, embrace our true identity and authority, we will realize that we are superior to the devil and his kingdom. Throughout the years, the church has received a bad name, but this was never a part of God's original plan. We were never meant to be a gathering of paupers but a gathering of kings and priests! Therefore, when we cast out demons, they must go!

My wife and I have dedicated our entire life and ministry to releasing people from the powers of darkness through this authority of which I speak. When we started our church several years ago, we began to rededicate the city of Tampa to God. The original name for Tampa was La Bahia de Espiritu Santo, or "The Bay of the Holy Spirit." Praise the Lord! Witches, warlocks, and demonic priests came from all around to destroy our ministry. As you may have guessed, they failed! Now we are giving the devil hell. You can, too!

Deliverance Prayer

Father, in the name of Jesus, I thank You for who You are and for all that You have done. Today, I declare that Your Word is the final authority in my life, and Your Word says that the kingdom of God lives inside my spirit. Through the power of the Holy Spirit, I purpose in my heart to advance the kingdom of God in every area of my life. I take authority over every curse, calamitous spirit, and demonic assignment, in Jesus' name. I am more than a conqueror through You, Lord Jesus. I loose myself from all lies of the evil one, especially those that suggest I am powerless, and I declare that I am filled with the power of God, fully equipped to carry out the Great Commission, according to Matthew 28:19. Thank You for granting me freedom in my mind, will, and emotions, in Jesus' name. Amen!

THE POSITION OF POWER

The centurion answered and said, Lord, I am not worthy that thou shouldest come under my roof: but speak the word only, and my servant shall be healed. For I am a man under authority, having soldiers under me: and I say to this man, Go, and he goeth; and to another, Come, and he cometh; and to my servant, Do this, and he doeth it.
—Matthew 8:8–9

As a ministry leader, I have consistently asked the Lord, "Why are so many people in the body of Christ bound by the enemy?" You may have realized by now that this has been a recurring theme of this book. The reason for this is that thousands of people have come to me seeking prayer for deliverance and restoration. Thousands desire to realize the abundant life that Jesus promised them in His Word.

We have spoken quite extensively on the subject of spiritual authority and the necessity of walking in dominion, but there is a component of spiritual authority that many people often neglect. It has never been a question of whether or not God's power is sufficient, or whether His Word is true. The real question is, Are you in the proper position?

Let me explain. In the eighth chapter of Matthew's gospel, Jesus encounters a centurion whose servant was grievously sick and tormented. Jesus told the centurion that He would come and heal the servant, but the centurion told Him it wasn't necessary; He need only speak the word, and the servant would be healed. (See Matthew 8:8.) The centurion backed up his confidence that the healing could happen in spite of the distance between his servant and Jesus with these words: *"For I am a man under authority...."* Jesus marveled at the centurion's faith. Why? Because, for the first time, Jesus had met someone who understood the dynamics of true authority.

WE CANNOT OPERATE IN AUTHORITY AND DOMINION UNTIL WE LEARN TO SUBMIT TO GOD.

Unlike this centurion, many people in the body of Christ are ignorant of the way biblical authority operates. They are not submitted to God's government in their lives; as a result, they are unable to walk in real freedom.

What did the centurion mean when he told Jesus, *"For I am a man under authority"*? He was saying, in essence, "I am a man who recognizes and submits to government." He recognized the authority of Jesus because he was a man under authority. He understood the power of authority. He knew that a person of authority needs only to say the word, and whatever he has ordered will happen.

As a result of his submission to natural government, the centurion was in a position to submit to the spiritual government of God. Many people in the church are not submitted to God, with the result being that they cannot exercise spiritual authority over the powers of darkness. Remember, all authority is delegated from one person to another. When you operate as a rogue agent, you have no authority! There are millions of Christians all over the world who have no regard for the spiritual authority of leaders in the body of Christ. They are not submitted to any pastor or spiritual leader, and this makes them vulnerable to the attacks of the devil. If you want to win the spiritual battles in your life, you must first learn to come under godly authority. Even Satan's kingdom is highly organized. The devil and his demons recognize rank, hierarchy, and structure.

Who's the Boss?

You may have heard the expression "Who's the boss?" The purpose of this question is to get us to examine who is really in charge of a given situation. Are you the king of your own castle, or is Jesus the King? This is a crucial question to answer, for without a proper understanding of, and submission to, biblical authority, you will experience chaos and destruction of satanic origins in your life.

Recall that in the first chapter of Genesis, the first thing God did was bring order out of chaos. He said, "Let there be light!" and dispelled the darkness. This was God's way of aligning everything in creation with His divine purposes. Yet I have met many believers whose lives are in total chaos and disorder, all because they refuse to accept the fact that they are not the bosses of their own lives.

The moment we came to faith in Christ, we professed Jesus as Lord, with the implication that we were no longer the lords of our own lives. The Greek word for "lord" is *kurios*, which means "landlord," or master; one who is "supreme in authority." Is Jesus the supreme authority in your life? Is He your Master? If so, then you can no longer make your own decisions and choices apart from Him. Your life belongs to Jesus! Yes, you may continue to exercise free will, but you must learn to consistently submit your will to His. After all, His will has your best interests at heart.

Your body, mind, money, and time—all that you are, and all that you have—belong to Him. Too many people are operating as spiritual vagabonds in the kingdom of God, never being settled or established, never being fathered or mothered by legitimate spiritual parents. This is the kind of situation the devil delights in, for he knows that once we stray away from our Shepherd, we will be exposed to his heinous attacks.

JESUS CAN DELIVER ONLY THOSE WHO SUBMIT WHOLEHEARTEDLY TO HIS LORDSHIP.

Many people want Jesus to be their deliverer, but they don't want to make Him Lord of their lives. Yet there is no real freedom or deliverance apart from the lordship of Jesus Christ. God does not set us free simply for us to brag about our own freedom. No, the Spirit of the Lord liberates us so that we can worship God in spirit and in truth. (See John 4:23–24.) I have found that many believers have been unable to escape various addictions because their motives for quitting are wrong. The only legitimate motive for freedom that pleases God is a desire to serve Him with one's whole heart.

Saints, we must examine ourselves! I know countless Christians who refuse to join a church or connect with a spiritual leader and come under his or her authority. This is spiritual insanity! I had a conversation with one man who asked me, "Do you have members at your church?" When I replied, "Of course!" he responded, "Then I can't be a part of your church. I don't want to be a part of any church that has members." It is this type of attitude that opens people up to the oppression of the devil.

The Bible clearly says that we should *"not [forsake] the assembling of ourselves together, as the manner of some is; but [should exhort] one another: and so much the more, as ye see the day approaching"* (Hebrews 10:25). The word *"assembling"* comes from the Greek word *episunagōgē*, which means "a gathering together." There is a corporate anointing available in the local body of believers that has the power to release people from bondage. God has called us to assemble together on a consistent basis for our mutual benefit. I know that many people have been wounded by their local church, but this is not a legitimate excuse to forsake God's ordinance to come together. Bring yourself under godly authority and watch the positive change that it makes.

Breaking the Spirit of Rebellion

All of us, even the sincerest of believers, have a tendency to rebel against God's Word. This is the by-product of our fallen humanity. However, if we have truly been born again, we will consistently examine our hearts to ensure that we are in proper alignment with the will of God. We must bring our flesh under subjection to the Word of God, in order to be less prone to fall prey to the spirit of rebellion.

The book of 1 Samuel provides a sober warning about rebellion. Addressing King Saul concerning his disobedience of God's command to totally destroy the Amalekites, the prophet Samuel said, *"For rebellion is as the sin of witchcraft, and stubbornness is as iniquity and idolatry. Because thou hast rejected the word of the Lord, he hath also rejected thee from being king"* (1 Samuel 15:23). In refusing to obey the Lord, King Saul was operating in a spirit of rebellion.

What is a spirit of rebellion? "Rebellion" is defined as "an act of violent or open resistance to an established government or ruler." Now that we agree on what constitutes rebellion, we can conclude that a spirit of rebellion is a demonic spirit that incites a person to reject God's government and rule in his or her life.

The devil loves rebels because they are a reflection of his prideful nature. The devil was kicked out of heaven because he defied the government and authority of God. Thus, whenever we are operating in a spirit of rebellion, we are emulating the devil. As a pastor, I can testify that people who operate in a spirit of rebellion consistently find themselves facing demonic oppression.

THE SPIRIT OF REBELLION SEDUCES A PERSON INTO BELIEVING HE OR SHE CAN MANIPULATE GOD'S WORD TO FIT HIS OR HER PREFERENCES IN A GIVEN SITUATION.

Oftentimes, we think that coming under authority—even that of God's government—is a sign of weakness. Yet submitting to God is actually an indicator of great strength. The enemy does not want us to yield to God, because he desires to isolate us in order to bring us into captivity. I often speak to people who complain about the demonic oppression they are facing. In most instances, the people who are experiencing the most severe demonic activity are living in rebellion.

Many years ago, I was praying for a married couple who were involved in our ministry at the time. They came to my wife and me and said that nothing we were teaching was working in their lives. Both the husband and the wife were experiencing severe demonic oppression. I became very frustrated and discouraged, so I went to God and asked Him what the problem was. I questioned Him as to why this couple was not experiencing victory. To my surprise, the Holy Spirit answered me, "They are not doing what you have told them to do!" He showed me that they were going through the religious motions but were not truly being obedient to God's Word. They wanted to experience the blessings of God without conforming to His will.

Later, I discovered that the couple had been engaged in all sorts of sinful activities, including witchcraft. How can someone expect to be free if he or she doesn't obey God's instructions? Rebels refuse to obey the Word of God. They reject accountability in their lives. They may even say that they will submit to God but not to a pastor, failing to realize that spiritual authority is always expressed through a human agency. If you can't submit to your pastor, how can you submit to God?

Again, the Bible equates rebellion with witchcraft. Why? Because people who are operating in rebellion are actually under the demonic influence of witchcraft and are ultimately practicing idolatry. Who is the object of their idol worship? The answer is, of course, themselves.

Submit to God and Resist the Devil

It may seem like a paradox to some, but the position of submission is the position of power. The Bible says, *"Submit yourselves therefore to God. Resist the devil, and he will flee from you"* (James 4:7). The word *"submit"* comes from the Greek word *hupotassō*—to "be... in subjection (to, under)." Before we can be in a position to resist the devil, we first must come under the control of the Holy Spirit.

Authority recognizes authority. The enemy knows whether or not you are under the authority of heaven. I want you to imagine a police officer. He or she has been given authority by the local governing body to arrest criminals and enforce the law. Yet this authority figure can function only if he or she is in right standing with the agency he or she represents. If the officer is suspended from his or her position, he or she no longer has the legal authority to arrest criminals. In essence, he or she has returned to being a normal citizen.

The same is true in the spiritual realm. If you and I are not submitted to God, we will not be able to operate in the authority God has given us to resist the devil. Many people are in partnership and agreement with the devil in their daily lives. These same people are frustrated when they rebuke the enemy but he doesn't flee. Submission is all about aligning oneself with the Word of God. When you and I come under the control of God's Word, we can rest assured that when we speak, the demons will flee.

SUBMISSION POSTURES US TO RELEASE THE AUTHORITY AND POWER OF HEAVEN IN OUR LIVES.

If you are battling a particular sin—lust, for example—the best way to overcome that sin is to bring your thought-life under subjection to the Word of God. This is done by taking lustful thoughts captive when they enter the mind. (See 2 Corinthians 10:5.) Every time the enemy of your soul sows a lustful thought in your mind, you should declare something like, "In the name of Jesus Christ, I cast down this ungodly imagination, and I take that wicked thought captive, in Jesus' name. I command you, devil, to go from me now!" If, on the other hand, you refuse to bring your thought-life under the dominion of God's Word, you will find it nearly impossible to win the battle in your mind.

You can see, then, that submission to the Word of God is for your benefit. The problem is that our society looks down on submission, particularly in the Western world. We promote freedom of expression and personal opinion above all else. Though freedom is a wonderful thing, we will never achieve true, lasting freedom until we have learned to submit to God.

At one point in my life, I myself struggled with lust. I had been exposed to pornography at an early age, and although I was not addicted to pornography, I struggled tremendously in my thought-life. This went on until, one day, the Lord revealed to me that I had never surrendered my whole mind to Him. I had reserved areas of my thought-life that were subconsciously closed off to the lordship of Jesus.

Beloved, you must understand that God wants all of you—not just the areas that are convenient. The Lord told me that He wanted to take control of my thoughts. I finally surrendered my mind to Him, and when I did, I was in a position to successfully resist the lustful thoughts that the enemy tried to plant in my mind.

This doesn't mean that the devil no longer attempts to attack my mind, but it does mean that I have a stronger defense because my mind is submitted to God. In fact, I have the mind of Christ! (See 1 Corinthians 2:16.) Hallelujah to the Lamb!

By Grace You Are Saved

There has been much conversation on the subject of grace in recent years. Many influential and extremely gifted teachers have expounded on God's unmerited favor toward His children. Honestly, I find most of the grace teaching to be very refreshing—it brings a wonderful balance to the legalistic doctrines that prevailed within the body of Christ for many years. On the other hand, grace must be understood in its proper biblical context if we are going to enjoy the powerful benefits that God intended for grace to produce in our lives.

There are some who present grace in a way that gives believers the license to sin or that understates the importance of obedience.

This is very dangerous! Grace is a crucial component of spiritual warfare. Why is it so important? The Bible says, *"For **by grace are ye saved** through faith; and that not of yourselves: it is the gift of God"* (Ephesians 2:8). When we look at salvation from the perspective of spiritual warfare, we are not just talking about walking down to an altar and confessing Christ as Lord.

The biblical term for "salvation" is the Greek term *sōzō*, which means "to...deliver or protect...heal, preserve,...be (make) whole." Simply put, salvation is deliverance. And what is the catalyst for this deliverance? The Bible says that we are saved by grace—the Greek word *charis*—or "the divine influence upon the heart, and its reflection in the life." In other words, grace is more than a response to our sin; it is the supernatural power that God grants His children to overcome the forces of darkness. Grace enables us to break free from addiction, depression, and even fear.

GRACE IS NOT A LICENSE TO SIN BUT IS RATHER THE SUPERNATURAL POWER OF GOD MADE AVAILABLE TO US, THAT WE MIGHT OVERCOME THE POWER OF SIN.

What does grace have to do with spiritual warfare? The Bible says, "[God] *giveth more grace. Wherefore he saith, God resisteth the proud, but giveth grace unto the humble"* (James 4:6). The word for *"grace"* in this verse is the same one that's found in Ephesians 2:8. Notice that the grace of God is not static; it is experienced to different degrees, depending on our humility. The Bible says that God resists the proud. He hates pride!

The word *"proud"* comes from the Greek word *huperēphanos*, and it relates to self-reliance. Those who refuse to submit to the rule and government of God, opting instead to rely upon their own gifts, talents, and merits, are preventing the grace of God from flowing in their lives. Those in a position to receive (i.e., in a posture of humility) will experience more of God's supernatural power, which is available to address any and all needs in their lives. I can't tell you how many people I have ministered to who could not be delivered, simply because they refused to humble themselves.

Grace is not passive; it is active. Are you experiencing spiritual resistance in your life? It could be the result of pride! It is crucial that we submit every area of our lives to God if we want to win against the enemy. We submit to God by obeying His Word and surrendering to His will. In this era of grace, we don't talk much about obedience, but obedience is key to living a victorious life. You may feel that you are incapable of obeying God in a certain area, but you must remember that God has already given you the grace to obey. All you need to do is humble yourself and open your heart to receive, and the supernatural power of God will flood your soul. Those things that had you bound won't be able to keep you bound any longer!

Deliverance Prayer

Father, in the name of Jesus, I declare that I am submitted to the lordship of Jesus Christ. I believe that Jesus is the Son of the living God, and that He suffered on the cross, died, and rose again, thereby defeating Satan. I also affirm that Jesus is now seated at the right hand of the Father. As an act I my free will, I submit myself to the Lord Jesus. The Bible tells me to submit to God and resist the devil; therefore; I declare that I am submitted to God in every area of my life. I take authority over the foul spirit of rebellion and over any instances of witchcraft. I actively resist any and all forms of rebellion that may be operating in my life right now. I renounce my right to exalt self above the Word of God, and I reject the temptation to yield to a spirit of haughtiness. In Jesus' name, I declare that any form of witchcraft operating in my life through rebellion, whether consciously or unconsciously, is broken right now! I am not ignorant of the devices of the devil. Holy Spirit, I grant You unconditional permission to guard my thoughts and emotions from the attacks of the enemy, in Jesus' name. Amen!

11

BREAKING DEMONIC STRONGHOLDS

> *For though we walk in the flesh, we do not war after the flesh: (for the weapons of our warfare are not carnal, but mighty through God to the pulling down of strong holds;) casting down imaginations, and every high thing that exalteth itself against the knowledge of God, and bringing into captivity every thought to the obedience of Christ.*
> —2 Corinthians 10:3–5

During my first trip to Israel, I had the opportunity to visit a famous landmark near the Dead Sea called Masada. In the year A.D. 66, Jewish Zealots took control of this desert stronghold overlooking the Dead Sea. The purpose of this stronghold was to protect the king in case of an enemy invasion. Some sources say that there were enough victuals inside the fortress to last its inhabitants for up to seven years.

In the year A.D. 73, the Roman governor Lucius Flavius Silva, with the aid of fifteen thousand Roman soldiers, laid siege to Masada. This was the last Jewish stronghold after the destruction of the temple in A.D. 70. The Roman soldiers had four outposts surrounding the mountain, and it took the Romans months to build a land bridge to the top of the mountain, where they could then use a battering ram to penetrate the walls.

Their efforts were hampered by stones thrown by the Zealots, killing several men who were working on the bridge; but finally, in the spring of A.D. 73, the Romans penetrated the walls of Masada. When they entered the fortress, however, they discovered that the Jewish Zealots had already committed suicide.

Today, Masada lies in ruins. Visiting this site gave me greater insight to the power of demonic strongholds. The Bible tells us that the weapons of our warfare are not carnal (physical) but are mighty through God to the pulling down of strongholds. The term *"strong holds"* in 2 Corinthians 10:4 comes from the Greek word *ochurōma*, which means "castle," or fortress. Just as in the case of Masada, the prince of this age has constructed strongholds in the lives of many believers—forts where he hides out and uses as a headquarters from which to launch his insidious schemes.

STRONGHOLDS ARE DEMONIC FORTRESSES ERECTED BY THE POWERS OF DARKNESS.

From a spiritual standpoint, demonic strongholds are established for the sole purpose of keeping people in captivity. These strongholds often manifest as thoughts, attitudes, and arguments in the mind that are resistant or hostile toward the Word of God. Strongholds may also take the form of sickness, disease, and infirmity.

The reason why many people are unable to break demonic strongholds in their lives is due to the fact that they are ignorant of the way strongholds work. When the enemy erects a stronghold, he always fortifies and defends his position. Wherever you identify a stronghold in your life, you can rest assured that the devil has no intention of leaving. When Masada was built, it was intended to be a long-term military fortress.

This is why the Bible says that strongholds must be pulled down. The phrase *"pulling down"* in 2 Corinthians 10:4 comes from the Greek word *kathairesis*, which means "destruction" or "demolition." The only way to get rid of a stronghold in your life is to demolish it through the supernatural power of the Word of God. Just like the Romans took a battering ram and broke down the walls of the desert fortress, so you and I must take the battering ram of the Word of God and break through the walls of oppression that have been erected in our lives by the powers of darkness.

Our Weapons Are Mighty Through God

The key to winning any battle is possessing a stronger arsenal than your enemy. Did you know that our weapons are more powerful than all the implements in the devil's arsenal? I like the way the *Amplified Bible* translates 2 Corinthians 10:4:

> *For the weapons of our warfare are not physical [weapons of flesh and blood], but they are mighty before God for the overthrow and destruction of strongholds.*

The word *"mighty"* comes from the Greek word *dunatos*, which means "able," "powerful or capable" and "strong." The spiritual weapons God has entrusted to us are powerful enough to break down any stronghold. You may be dealing with strongholds of fear, shame, and condemnation. Beloved, I have good news for you—you need not be a victim! Let me remind you once more: *"Greater is he that is in you, than he that is in the world"* (1 John 4:4).

Have you ever witnessed a building being demolished? If you haven't, it is definitely a sight to see! The process often involves a wrecking ball—a large sphere of solid steel that is suspended from a crane. The weight of the ball combined with the momentum from the crane, creates the force necessary to destroy almost any infrastructure in its path. Beloved, the Word of God is the wrecking ball of the spiritual realm, capable of bringing destruction to any demonic stronghold in the life of a believer. The more we read, meditate on, and obey the Word of God, the more spiritual momentum is created to pull down strongholds.

THE ENEMY IS TERRIFIED OF YOUR REALIZING HOW POWERFUL YOU REALLY ARE.

Every stronghold is surrounded by a structure called a bulwark, or rampart, whose purpose is to protect the occupants of the stronghold. For this purpose, bulwarks are heavily guarded. Have you ever wondered why it seems that the harder you strive to break free in certain areas of your life, the more the spiritual opposition intensifies? This is because the devil is feeling the pressure and strengthening the bulwarks around the strongholds he has erected in your life.

It is for this reason that the Bible tells us to "pull down," or demolish, demonic strongholds. The longer they go unchecked, the stronger they become. Every day that you allow the enemy to attack and torment you is another day that he has to tighten his stranglehold on your life.

The Bible says that we are to "[cast] *down imaginations, and every high thing that exalteth itself against the knowledge of God, and* [bring] *into captivity every thought to the obedience of Christ*" (2 Corinthians 10:5). Notice that the apostle Paul used another strong phrase, *"casting down"—kathaireō* in Greek, meaning "extinction," "destruction." The idea is that we must use extreme force in order to throw down the bulwarks of the devil.

The problem is, too many believers are lazy! When they don't see instant results, they become frustrated and discouraged and quickly give up. This is not the right way to approach a stronghold. You must recognize that this is a spiritual fight—one that will require persistence and resilience until you see the results that God has promised you.

The bulwarks of the enemy are imaginations or strands of logical reasoning that are hostile toward God. These imaginations manifest as fear, doubt, unbelief, and discouragement. They tell you that you will never be delivered from anxiety, lust, or other oppressive torments. The devil is a liar! You can be free today, but you must be willing to take a stand.

Learning to Identify Strongholds

We've established that the average believer isn't likely to realize when he or she is dealing with a demonic stronghold. What are the identifying features of a spiritual stronghold in your life? If you are struggling with a pervasive sin or addiction, you may be dealing with a demonic stronghold. If there is a chronic sickness that seems to "run in your family," then you may be dealing with a demonic stronghold. When you have gone to the altar several times for prayer and still can't manage to break free from bondage, the enemy may have established a fortress in your life. By definition, strongholds are persistent, debilitating, long-lasting, hostile, and oppressive. Some examples of demonic strongholds include unrelenting sickness, life-controlling addictions, poverty, sexual perversion, spiritual stagnation, mental illness, emotional turmoil, depression, anxiety, and fear. This list is not exhaustive, by any means, but it is meant to help you know when to suspect that a stronghold may be operating in your life or in the lives of those you love.

Remember, you will never break the power of a stronghold unless you first identify it as such. Unfortunately, many people continue making excuses for the demonic activity in their lives—some of them under the encouragement of leaders within the body of Christ!

As a pastor, I have helped countless people in their efforts to break free from the demonic strongholds in their lives. Many of them have been successfully liberated, but some have gotten offended by the suggestion that they might have a stronghold of demonic activity in their life; therefore, they remain in bondage. They fail to recognize that the offense they take at my offer to help is, itself, a bulwark of the enemy.

ASK GOD TO OPEN YOUR EYES IN THE SPIRIT SO THAT YOU WILL BE ABLE TO IDENTIFY ANY STRONGHOLDS THAT SATAN MAY HAVE ESTABLISHED IN YOUR LIFE.

You must remember that Satan is empowered by anonymity. He hides his activities within the deep recesses of our thoughts, attitudes, and behaviors. This is why so many people are unable to identify demonic strongholds—because those strongholds are often interwoven within the fabric of their mind.

Again, the Bible tells us to cast down imaginations and every high thing that exalts itself against the knowledge of God. (See 2 Corinthians 10:5.) The word *"imaginations"* in this verse comes from the Greek word *logismos*, which means "computation" or "reasoning." In other words, these imaginations are demonic thoughts that conceal themselves as logical arguments in the mind of the believer, when, in fact, they are hostile barriers used by the devil to guard the strongholds he has established. Simply put, the enemy of your soul tries to establish logical barriers in your mind that will justify your captivity.

At a recent book signing, I met a man who began to argue with me about the reality of divine healing. He asserted that healing was not for today. This gentleman, bless his soul, had been trained in seminary; he knew how to read and speak Greek, but he was afflicted by sickness. The enemy was using wicked imaginations in the form of reason and logic to justify his sickness to himself, thereby keeping him bound.

Beloved, we cannot allow the enemy to deceive us! We must cast down every sequence of logical reasoning that would keep us from walking in the freedom and peace that God has ordained for our lives. Break through the barrier of pride, reason, logic, and intellectualism, and renew your mind with the Word of God today!

Dethroning Dark Princes

It is important to understand that strongholds are not empty infrastructures; they are dense constructs meant to house someone or something. In other words, strongholds are residential fortresses. Ephesians 2:2 says, *"In time past ye walked according to the course of this world, according to the prince of the power of the air, the spirit that now worketh in the children of disobedience."* In this verse, Satan is referred to as the *"prince of the power of the air."* What does this phrase mean? For *"prince,"* the apostle Paul uses the Greek word *archon*, which means "chief," "magistrate," or "ruler." The word *"air,"* as used here, refers to the atmospheric region or expanse. In other words, Satan is the commander and ruler of the power in the atmospheric region.

It is commonly taught that the devil and the demonic hosts inhabit hell, when, in fact, they populate the atmosphere, or the "second heaven." Satan's goal is to manipulate the communication that we receive, whether over the radio, on television, by computer, or through any other form of media that is transmitted over the air. He controls the mind-sets and thought patterns of cities, nations, territories, and regions.

Have you ever wondered why certain cities or regions seem to deal with a pervasive sin or problematic issue, such as crime, racism, or poverty? The truth is that the enemy has established spiritual fortresses in these communities, which give him access to the thoughts and minds of the people living there. The enemy's agenda is to rule and reign in the lives and minds of those who will yield to his deception.

THE DEVIL'S AGENDA IS NOT MERELY BONDAGE AND CAPTIVITY BUT ALSO COMPLETE RULE AND DOMINATION.

Since the devil has no intention of letting go of his control, it's up to us to dethrone the enemy in every area of our lives. Remember, the devil is full of pride and desires to be worshipped and exalted above anything else. How do we dethrone the enemy? By following the apostle Paul's exhortation in 2 Corinthians 10:5 and taking every thought captive to the obedience of Christ. The more we walk in obedience to the Word of God, the weaker the influence of the wicked one becomes.

Many people think that the term "obedience" is legalistic, but nothing could be further from the truth. In fact, you will never live a life of freedom until you learn to obey God's Word. Whether you realize it or not, God has already granted you the power and the authority to cast out the devil.

One of the simplest, most powerful ways to walk in obedience is through prayer and intercession. Prayer has the power to dislodge the grip of Satan on your mind. Every time we come to God in faith and make supplication to Him, the fingers of the enemy are broken.

When my wife and I first moved to Tampa, I discerned that there was a strong spirit of religion there that had erected a stronghold in the minds of the people. The prevailing attitude toward God and His kingdom was apathy and indifference. The Holy Spirit told us to pray that the stronghold of religion would be broken. Now, after many years of praying that prayer, we are seeing thousands of people being set free from the stranglehold of dead religion and empty tradition. We have dethroned the prince of the power of the air and have dedicated our city to the Lord Jesus Christ.

You can do the same in your mind, your family, your community, and your city. You can cast down every demonic imagination, mind-set, and attitude that is contrary to the Word of God, and declare that Jesus is Lord. God is waiting on you to stand up and resist the devil. Let me be clear: The Lord Jesus Christ has already dethroned the devil—his ultimate end is destruction—but we must enforce this reality in our lives on a daily basis.

Stopping the Spirit of Leviathan

So far, we have talked extensively about the nature of strongholds and the tools necessary to tear them down. Still, the fact remains that plenty of Spirit-filled people who know the Word and attend church regularly continue to struggle with life-controlling issues and mental strongholds. I have watched plenty of earnest, well-meaning Christians come to the altar for healing and deliverance, only to find themselves still trapped in captivity. Do these people not love God? Is there faith not sincere?

I'll acknowledge that there are those who are insincere in their faith and devotion to the Lord Jesus, but it is my impression that most born-again believers have a genuine desire to please God.

Enter a mysterious yet significant creature mentioned in the Bible: leviathan.

> *In that day the LORD with his sore and great and strong sword shall punish leviathan the piercing serpent, even leviathan that crooked serpent; and he shall slay the dragon that is in the sea.* (Isaiah 27:1)

A leviathan is another word for "serpent," "sea monster," or "dragon." In the Bible, leviathan is depicted as a large dragon or sea creature. Though there are many theories about this creature, the most important thing to understand is what leviathan represents: pride, perversion, and haughtiness. In short, the spirit of leviathan is the spirit of pride—a spirit that is keeping many people in the church bound up in captivity.

THE SPIRIT OF PRIDE KEEPS US FOCUSED ON OURSELVES, SO THAT WE DON'T RELY COMPLETELY ON GOD FOR OUR FREEDOM AND DELIVERANCE.

This spirit can operate in the life of a believer subconsciously, motivating self-centeredness and affectation. You must understand that at the root of all depression, fear, anxiety, lust, and addiction is a vain concentration on self instead of on God. This principality of pride becomes a veritable sea monster or dragon in a person's life, lurking inconspicuously beneath the waters of good intentions. This spirit is "crooked" in that it twists reality, incites offense and hurt, and warps a person's perceptions of himself and others.

The Bible refers to leviathan as a *"piercing serpent."* This is the Hebrew word *bariyach*, which means "a fugitive," or "fleeing." A fugitive is someone who has fled or escaped and is now hiding to avoid capture and further persecution. This is the way that pride works. The average person would never admit to being prideful, because his pride is concealed by his own sense of spirituality and self-importance. But anytime we assume that God's Word does not work, or that what it says does not apply to us, we are harboring the fugitive spirit of pride.

The moment we embrace the truth of God's Word, the hold of leviathan is broken over our lives. The reason why this is so important is because pride will keep a person from receiving the deliverance that he or she so desperately needs. We must come to a place where we are willing to humble ourselves and take responsibility for our current status in life. We must admit that we are wrong and be willing to repent (i.e., change our mind). So many people are being oppressed because they won't admit their need of God's divine intervention. It's not God's fault! Remember, God resists the proud, but He gives grace to the humble. The moment you renounce your sense of self-importance and cry out to God, you posture yourself to receive His supernatural power and grace, which are far more powerful than any manifestation of the leviathan spirit.

Freedom from the Spirit of the Age

Have you ever wondered why it seems difficult for some believers to pray, fast, or read the Word of God on a consistent basis? Have you ever considered the reason for the intense warfare people encounter that keeps them from coming to church or committing wholeheartedly to the things of God? What about the lack of power that is prevalent in so many churches and denominations? We are living in a season in which secularism and spiritual compromise have attempted to exert their influence on the body of Christ. This is what we call the "spirit of the age."

In the book of 2 Timothy, the apostle Paul offers the following caution:

> *This know also, that in the last days perilous times shall come. For men shall be lovers of their own selves, covetous, boasters, proud, blasphemers, disobedient to parents, unthankful, unholy, without natural affection, trucebreakers, false accusers, incontinent, fierce, despisers of those that are good, traitors, heady, highminded, lovers of pleasures more than lovers of God; having a form of godliness, but denying the power thereof: from such turn away.* (2 Timothy 3:1–5)

This Scripture passage paints a very vivid picture of the spiritual state of many people today, even within the body of Christ. There are many believers who have a *"form of godliness,"* meanwhile denying the power of God. The apathy, selfishness, stagnancy, and worldliness that we see in the lives of so many Christians are manifestations of the spirit of the age.

The apostle John referred to this spirit by another name: the spirit of antichrist. (See 1 John 2:18; 4:3.) Contrary to popular belief, he was not referring to the Antichrist—a specific person who will appear at the end of the age—but rather a spirit, or influence, operating in the lives of many people inside the church. The word *antichrist* comes from the Greek word *antichristos*, which means "opponent of the Messiah" (the anointed one). This spirit is the driving force behind the humanistic philosophy that promotes Christianity without commitment, love without obedience, and forgiveness without repentance. I refer to this as "counterfeit Christianity"—a Christianity devoid of the love, power, and presence of almighty God, as well as a rejection of the truthfulness and validity of Scripture.

The only way that believers will be able to live free from the influence of the spirit of the age (the spirit of antichrist) is by receiving a supernatural revelation of the person, power, and nature of Jesus Christ. Once you have encountered the *real* Jesus, Satan will never be able to seduce you with his counterfeit again. I declare that you are free today from the spirit of the age, in Jesus' name!

Dismantling the Stronghold of Lack

Many years ago, my wife and I were plagued by serious financial struggles. There were times when we had to pray and believe God for the money to buy dinner. At one point, the situation became so dire that we went to our church pantry and filled up on chips and salsa. How did two college graduates living in the most prosperous country in the world come to experience such lack? The simple truth is that lack and poverty are not just social phenomena, they are demonic spirits.

You might think that tithing faithfully would have ended this vicious cycle, but it didn't. Remember, doing something with the wrong heart and the wrong attitude is often just as fruitless as if you didn't do it at all. What was the problem? We were bound by a spirit of poverty and didn't even realize it. And my sense of pride and inflated ego only made matters worse. Even though I knew the Word and what it has to say about the spirit of poverty, I couldn't seem to break free.

Finally, I realized that I needed to humble myself and ask God for help. So, I prayed to the Lord, "Teach me how to prosper!" This admission of need, born of desperation and humility, broke something inside me. The stronghold of lack in my mind began to crumble. I went to the Word and read every Scripture I could find on financial prosperity, quickly coming to realize that my knowledge on the subject wasn't as vast as I'd thought.

The more I meditated on the Word of God and obeyed what I read, the more I began to experience freedom from the poverty mentality. Eventually, I was completely set free and started enjoying the abundant life that Jesus paid for His children to enjoy.

Why do I share this story? I want you to know that you have a tremendous role to play in the dismantling of strongholds in your own life. First, you must humble yourself and determine in your heart that God's Word is the final authority in your life. Second, you must exercise the authority of the name of Jesus to break the spirit of pride, along with every other stronghold operating in your life.

Deliverance Prayer

Father, in the name of Jesus Christ, I come to You now as my Deliverer. You know the torment that I have experienced from spiritual strongholds in my life, and I recognize that You alone have the power to deliver me from them. In the name of Jesus, I take authority over the leviathan spirit and command pride, ego, arrogance, skepticism, and self-reliance to go from me, right now. I declare that through the shed blood of the Lamb, Jesus Christ, every addiction, bondage, and demonic stronghold in my life is broken! I submit to the lordship and direction of Jesus Christ, and I yield to the Holy Spirit as my Comforter, Teacher, and Empowerment to fulfill the divine assignment You have placed upon my life. Forgive me, Lord, for any area of sin, especially disobedience or pride, operating in my life, whether knowingly or unknowingly. I declare by faith that I am completely and totally free today! In Jesus' name, amen!

DISRUPTING THE ENEMY'S PATTERNS

Christ hath redeemed us from the curse of the law, being made a curse for us: for it is written, Cursed is every one that hangeth on a tree.
—Galatians 3:13

In an earlier chapter, we discussed how the transgression of Adam and Eve in the garden of Eden caused a ripple effect in the spiritual fabric of humanity. The pattern of sin, iniquity, and shame that they instituted has affected every generation of humanity. Unfortunately, many people are still trapped in this destructive pattern of the enemy.

The human proclivity toward sin was ushered in by the curse. Yet the Bible tells us that Christ has redeemed us from the curse of the law, having been made a curse for us. In other words, He has given us a way out!

A pattern is a regular, predictable form that typically repeats itself. You must understand that the kingdom of darkness follows a carefully crafted pattern of attack and conquest. Just as a military force has patterns and formations it employs when engaging in warfare, so the enemy of our souls has a predictable method of oppression and control. The best way to defeat an enemy on the battlefield is to disrupt his patterns. The devil is counting on your conforming to his pattern, or way of doing things. He believes that he has you figured out. Just like an architect drafts a blueprint for building, so the enemy lays out clandestine plans for your demise.

However, the enemy has not factored in the possibility of his demonic patterns being disrupted. How do we disrupt the enemy's patterns? The Bible commands us in Ephesians 4:27, *"Neither give place to the devil."* The word *"place"* comes from the Greek word *topos*, which refers to a specific space or station. Simply put, we must destroy the stations of the enemy that he has set up in our lives, most often in the mind. By closing off space to the enemy, you are frustrating his intentions.

YOU DON'T HAVE TO CONFORM TO THE SCHEMES AND DEVICES OF THE ENEMY ANYMORE. GIVE HIM NO PLACE!

We disrupt the devil's patterns through repentance of sins and through the renewal of our minds. Again, the Bible says, *"Be not conformed to this world: but be ye transformed by the renewing of your mind…"* (Romans 12:2). In other words, we must not conform to the pattern that the enemy has crafted for our lives, but rather be transformed by the renovating of our minds.

Can you imagine if someone entered your home while you were away and rearranged all your furniture? That would be very frustrating, to say the least. If you really want to offend the devil, rearrange the "furniture" in your mind—you'll throw him off his game! In those places where you were once susceptible to temptation, make the decision to refuse to yield to him any longer.

You will notice, if you pay close attention, that every failure in your life follows a pattern. Whether it is habitual sin, addiction, or fear, you must intentionally deviate from what you are accustomed to doing. If you want to experience a level of freedom that you have never enjoyed before, you must be willing to make drastic changes in your life. For example, if you are struggling with fear, you must change the things that you allow "in" through the gates of your eyes. If you are struggling with lust, guard your heart and relationships like never before. These are practical steps toward seeing the freedom that you desire. And it all begins with meditating on the Word of God and allowing it to transform your mind—to rearrange your mental furniture.

Breaking Ungodly Cycles

Now I'd like for you to imagine a carousel at an amusement park. You are riding this carousel, and it is spinning faster and faster. At some point, you want to get off the dizzying ride, but you can't; it is spinning out of control. What started out as amusement has quickly turned into nausea and terror.

The scenario that I have just described aptly summarizes the experience common to countless people in the body of Christ—well-meaning Christians who are trapped in an ungodly cycle, whether one of fear, addiction, self-hatred, disobedience, or something else.

We have been entertaining these questions: Why are so many people unable to live the life that God has ordained for them? Why are so many saints bound, bitter, and broken? The truth is, they are caught up in the devil's "carousel ride." They are trapped in a cycle—a series of events that are repetitive in nature. Cycles are often pervasive and trans-generational, meaning that they are passed down from one generation to the next.

An example of a trans-generational cycle of sin is that of generational curses, such as domestic abuse, molestation, poverty, failed marriages, and even suicide. But take heart—the Bible says that we have been redeemed from the curse. Not only has the curse of sin been broken by Jesus Christ, but we have also received the blessing of Abraham. (See Galatians 3:13–14.) The blessing is far more powerful than the curse!

THE ONLY WAY TO BREAK AN UNGODLY CYCLE IS BY INVOKING THE POWER OF THE BLOOD OF JESUS AND DECLARING THE BLESSING.

Even though the curse of sin was broken on the cross, we must insist upon our new covenant rights if we want to break the ungodly cycles in our lives. The devil would have us going around in circles, year in, year out. He wants us to repeat the cycle of sin, shame, and condemnation. I don't know about you, but I refuse to perpetuate any cyclical patterns of oppression! Remember, when you have been washed in the blood of Jesus Christ, Satan no longer has the legal right to oppress you. Therefore, the only way he can continue to oppress you is with your permission.

The more you declare God's Word over your mind and subconscious, the more you will release the power of the blessing in your life. Take note of the enemy's patterns. What happens before you give in to a particular temptation? How do you feel right before you commit that particular sin? Paying attention to these details will help you to identify the catalysts for certain sinful patterns in your life.

For example, many sexual sins are connected to feelings of loneliness. Oftentimes, people find themselves most tempted by sexual sin when they are feeling abandoned or alone. The moment you identify the root cause of a particular sinful tendency, you can begin to take authority over the demonic influences that are drawing you into it. Before you yield to your fleshly desires, declare, for example, "I am not alone, because the Holy Spirit is my Comforter and Friend! Spirit of lust, I command you to go from me now, in Jesus' name!"

The Bible commands us in Romans 6:12, *"Let not sin therefore reign in your mortal body, that ye should obey it in the lusts thereof."* The truth is that God has already empowered you with the grace necessary to break any and every ungodly cycle affecting your life. You can do all things through Christ who gives you strength. (See Philippians 4:13.) It is time for you to break free!

Identifying and Breaking Curses

Earlier, we introduced the concept of curses—specifically, generational curses. Now I would like to talk about curses in general. What is a curse, exactly? From a biblical standpoint, the word "curse" refers to an imprecation of evil or a solemn utterance. The word for *"curse"* in the New Testament is derived from the Greek word *katara*, which means "imprecation, execration." Simply stated, a curse is any malevolent supernatural force (usually expressed in a verbal utterance, whether audible or not) working in a person's life, which produces calamity, destruction, or harm.

There are three agencies capable of pronouncing curses: God, the devil, and human beings. In our discussion of generational curses, we explored this Scripture from the Old Testament, which describes God as…

> *Keeping mercy for thousands, forgiving iniquity and transgression and sin, and that will by no means clear the guilty; visiting the iniquity of the fathers upon the children, and upon the children's children, unto the third and to the fourth generation.* (Exodus 34:7)

God promised to visit the iniquities of the fathers upon their children—a generational curse. However, the book of Ezekiel records the following:

> *The soul that sinneth, it shall die. The son shall not bear the iniquity of the father, neither shall the father bear the iniquity of the son: the righteousness of the righteous shall be upon him, and the wickedness of the wicked shall be upon him.*
>
> (Ezekiel 18:20)

This means that, for the born-again believer, God is not the agent responsible for curses. The pattern of visiting the iniquities of the fathers on their children has been broken through the shed blood of Jesus. (See Galatians 3:13.) If God is not the one responsible for curses, then who is? I would argue that Satan is the one who seeks to curse God's people. Much to the devil's chagrin, he cannot successfully curse whom God has blessed. How is it, then, that there are many believers living under a curse, even while God says they are blessed? It is because they are ignorant.

Remember what God said in Hosea 4:6:

> *My people are destroyed for lack of knowledge: because thou hast rejected knowledge, I will also reject thee, that thou shalt be no priest to me: seeing thou hast forgotten the law of thy God, I will also forget thy children.*

Even though Christ has redeemed us from the curse, we must know and insist upon the blessing in order experience its benefits. If we don't know that we are blessed in Christ, Satan will continue to perpetuate the curse in our lives.

SATAN DESIRES TO CURSE GOD'S PEOPLE THROUGH THEIR UNKNOWING PARTNERSHIP AND AGREEMENT.

Unfortunately, many believers are "aiding and abetting" the devil and his curses by the words they speak. Remember, a curse is essentially a verbal pronouncement of evil on someone (including oneself). For instance, a parent can speak a curse over his or her children. A pastor can pronounce a curse over his or her congregation. People often speak things over themselves that can produce devastating effects on their lives, such as "I will never get better!" or "I will never have any money!"

These are examples of curses spoken over self and others. When evil words are spoken, it sets spiritual forces in motion that have the power to alter the framework of your life. These words give permission to the enemy to act.

How do we identify when a curse is at work in our lives? If you find yourself in a state of constant chaos, calamity, and turmoil, you may be operating under a curse. Some other examples of curses include unexplained illness, premature death, mental strongholds, severe and/or consistent loss, and extreme poverty. I am not suggesting that Christians be superstitious or fearful, blaming everything on curses; but it is very important for us to know how to identify when a curse is in operation.

Once a curse has been identified, it can easily be broken. How do you break a demonic curse? The first step in neutralizing curses in our lives is by pronouncing the blessing. Remember, curses are words! If you want to change what you are experiencing, then you must change what you are speaking. The second step in breaking curses is ceasing to agree with them and renouncing any participation with curses. You must make a conscious decision to lay the ax to the root of anything in your life that is sabotaging your destiny.

You may be thinking to yourself, *But I thought you said the curse was broken!* The curse *was* broken, and you do have authority over the powers of darkness; but you must *exercise spiritual dominion* in order to live free from the implications of the curse. Too many people are unintentionally perpetuating the effects of the curse in their own lives. When you truly realize the price Jesus paid for your freedom, you will insist that all illegal activity in your life come to an end, in Jesus' name. Remember, the blessing is greater than the curse!

Releasing Supernatural Breakthrough

As I mentioned previously, I know from firsthand experience what it is to be bound. I have felt the weight of shame and guilt that comes from sinning against God, especially when we have promised Him never to commit that particular sin again. Not only have I experienced this, but also I have ministered to thousands of people who are struggling with similar manifestations of bondage. If you are sick and tired of being sick and tired, and if you're ready to break free, the Spirit of the Lord wants to liberate you right now! You must understand, however, that there is a significant difference between being inconvenienced by your sin and being ready for a change. It is only when we are truly ready to experience change and transformation in our lives that we can achieve spiritual breakthrough.

In the book of Micah, we find a relevant passage:

> *I will surely assemble, O Jacob, all of thee; I will surely gather the remnant of Israel; I will put them together as the sheep of Bozrah, as the flock in the midst of their fold: they shall make great noise by reason of the multitude of men. The breaker is come up before them: they have broken up, and have passed through the gate, and are gone out by it: and their king shall pass before them, and the LORD on the head of them.*
>
> (Micah 2:12–13)

The term *"Bozrah"* is significant; it comes from the Hebrew word *botsrah*, which means "enclosure" or "sheepfold." Bozrah was the capital city of Jordan, and it was widely known as a shepherd city. Why is Bozrah significant to this conversation about breakthrough? It was a city that prophetically symbolized the bondage of God's people. Bozrah represents the captivity that many people in the body of Christ are experiencing today.

SUPERNATURAL BREAKTHROUGH IS THE DEMOLISHING OF BARRIERS, ADDICTIONS, AND HINDRANCES IN YOUR LIFE THROUGH THE POWER OF THE HOLY SPIRIT.

Micah 2:13 says, *"The breaker is come up before them."* What is the *"breaker"*? The word comes from the Hebrew term *parats*, which means to "break away" or "burst out." This is what I call the "breaker anointing." God released a prophetic word through the prophet Micah, telling him that He was about to send the "breaker" to His people so that they would no longer be in bondage and affliction but would "pass through the gate." The gate represents freedom, liberation, and spiritual breakthrough.

Have you ever felt stuck? Have you found yourself repeating the same cycle of defeat, over and over again? It is time for you to experience the breaker anointing! I am here to tell you, beloved, that God has already released His breaker anointing in and upon your life by the Holy Spirit, and you are about to come out of your captivity, in Jesus' name. Your "sheepfold" can no longer confine you, because God is releasing His people from bondage right now! You are about to come out like those sheep in Bozrah, and you will testify of the goodness of the Lord in the land of the living.

Many people who come to our church have battled illness, addictions, and defeat for years; others have long been oppressed by the spirit of dead religion and empty tradition. Nonetheless, most of them find themselves free and able to walk in the abundant life once they are exposed to the very teaching that I am sharing with you right now. The moment you recognize that the breaker anointing already resides in you, the devil will never be able to keep you in captivity again.

Testimonies of Breakthrough

I know a young man who struggled with sexual sin since he was five years old. His brother had introduced him to adult entertainment when he was very young. Although he was not involved in any sexual relationship, he was addicted to pornography, sexual lust, and perversion for many years. The turning point came when someone gave him a book on deliverance. He learned for the first time that pornography and sexual uncleanness were grave sins. Once he discovered this truth, he prayed a simple prayer, which he had learned from the deliverance manual: "Father, in the name of Jesus Christ, I expose my entire spirit, soul, and body to the blood of Jesus Christ, the Word of God, and the fire of the Holy Spirit. I command anything in me that was not planted by You to be uprooted, in Jesus' name. I speak to my conscious, subconscious, and unconscious mind and command it to be free from all lust, idolatry, and uncleanness, in the precious name of Jesus."

After praying that prayer, he began to yawn uncontrollably, after which he felt as if something was being lifted off of him. From that moment on, he was completely and totally delivered. To God be the glory! Whether he recognized it or not, he experienced supernatural breakthrough in his life. The beautiful part about this story is that if God worked deliverance for this young man, He will do the same for you. All that's required of you is to believe and trust God's Word. Acknowledge that God is more than able to deliver you and set you free from whatever is plaguing you today. In fact, I would submit to you that He has already delivered you—He did so over two thousand years ago, when Jesus

Christ died on the cross of Calvary and rose again. Now it is time for you to receive this finished work!

SUPERNATURAL BREAKTHROUGH IS RELEASED BY FAITH IN THE WORD OF GOD. IF YOU WILL SIMPLY BELIEVE, YOU WILL EXPERIENCE THE MANIFESTATION OF HIS POWER!

Another person testified that he had been severely addicted to cigarettes. He had tried every cure imaginable, to no avail. He would pray, line up for healing, and read the Bible; nothing seemed to work. As you can imagine, this person became very frustrated and discouraged. One evening, I was hosting a healing school, and this man was in attendance, desiring to receive prayer. The presence of God was very strong that night! I had no foreknowledge of this man's struggle; it was the Holy Spirit, through a word of knowledge, who prompted me to call forward for prayer people suffering with specific conditions and ailments.

When this young man came forward, I prayed a prayer of release and deliverance over him. Later, he contacted me to tell me that when I prayed for him, he had been instantly set free from his addiction to nicotine. In the days and weeks since, every time he would consider smoking, the taste for cigarettes would leave his mouth. He was completely and totally delivered through the power of the breaker anointing. Remember, the anointing destroys the yoke! It does not matter how long you have been bound; the power of the kingdom of God is always available to make you free.

Deliverance Prayer

Father, in the name of Jesus, I thank You for who You are and for all that You have done. Today, I declare that any and all curses afflicting my life and mind are broken. Every negative word that has been spoken over me, consciously or unconsciously, is now nullified, in the name of Jesus Christ. I renounce and cancel any negative words that I have spoken over myself and believed. I declare that I am blessed, in the name of Jesus, and I have a goodly heritage, according to Psalm 16:6. I speak crop failure to every word of defeat, failure, destruction, calamity, delay, regression, lack, worry, and unfruitfulness. I command every demonic portal that has opened the door to dysfunction, fear, depression, calamity, or death to be permanently closed, in Jesus' name. I declare that everything in my life is working toward my good, in accordance with Romans 8:28. I am blessed to be a blessing, in the name of Jesus Christ. Amen!

THE SHIELD OF FAITH

Above all, [take] the shield of faith, wherewith ye shall be able to quench all the fiery darts of the wicked.
—Ephesians 6:16

In chapter eight, we discussed the various components of our spiritual armor as listed by the apostle Paul in Ephesians 6:16. Now I would like to talk in greater depth about the *"shield of faith,"* which Paul admonishes us to take up *"above all."* The phrase "above all" denotes priority. The question is, What is faith, and why is it so important?

We find the answer in the book of Hebrews:

Faith is the substance of things hoped for, the evidence of things not seen.…But without faith it is impossible to please him [God]: for he that cometh to God must believe that he is, and that he is a rewarder of them that diligently seek him.
(Hebrews 11:1, 6)

The word *"faith"* in this passage is derived from the Greek word *pistis*, which means "conviction (of religious truth, or the truthfulness of God)"; "assurance, belief,...fidelity." In other words, the writer of Hebrews is saying, faith is the firm persuasion and confidence that God's Word is true.

Faith is one of the most important dimensions of the Christian life. It is *"the substance of things hoped for."* This phrase is summed up in the Greek word *hupostasis*, which means "assurance." In other words, faith is the "title deed" to every promise in the kingdom of God.

What does this have to do with spiritual warfare? Without confidence in God's Word, we have no defense against the attacks of the evil one.

FAITH IS THE SUPERNATURAL KEY TO RELEASING THE PROMISES AND POWER OF GOD IN YOUR LIFE.

Why does Paul refer to faith as a shield? We discussed this briefly in chapter eight, but I believe it's worth revisiting. In ancient Rome, legionnaires (Roman soldiers) were equipped with large shields to protect themselves from head to toe in battle. Usually, these shields were made of leather or animal hide. They were extremely durable and nearly impenetrable, just as our faith ought to be as we enter into spiritual battle.

The Bible says that with the shield of faith, *"ye shall be able to quench all the fiery darts of the wicked."* This is an allusion to the infamous "fiery darts" used during the time of the Roman Empire. A fiery dart was a spear soaked in a flammable liquid and launched into the formation of the enemy during battle. The Roman army was so advanced that they would saturate their shields in water, so that every time the flaming spears of their enemy were thrown, the wet shields would extinguish the flame.

This is the power of faith. Every time we declare the promises of God and stand on them by faith, we extinguish the fiery attacks of the kingdom of darkness. For example, the devil may be sending lying symptoms to your body, telling you that you are sick; but faith says, "I am the healed of the Lord, according to 1 Peter 2:24, which says that by the stripes of Jesus, I am healed." Hallelujah!

Your faith acts as a supernatural shield, guarding your soul and protecting your spiritual life from penetration by the enemy. This is why a proper understanding of faith is so critical when it comes to spiritual warfare. The authority that God has given us to resist the evil one operates by faith in the Word of God. You must trust what God says about you! You must believe in your heart that greater is the One who lives in you than all the forces of darkness that surround you. Every time you confess God's Word in faith, you put out yet another flaming dart from the enemy's camp.

The Just Shall Live by Faith

I cannot stress enough the importance of faith. It is the ultimate key to victorious living, because it gives us the confidence in God that we need in order to overcome the evil one. Without confidence in God, we would flounder hopelessly as victims of fear.

Too many people in the body of Christ are living in fear. Beloved, this is not God's will for His children. The Bible says, *"The just shall live by faith"* (Romans 1:17). He did not say, "The just shall live by fear." Those of us who have been called by God and justified through the atoning blood of His Son Jesus Christ have been ordained to live a life of faith.

Remember, fear is the culture of the kingdom of darkness, and it acts as fuel to energize demonic activity. Faith, on the other hand, is the driving force behind God's kingdom, and the catalyst through which His power is released. If we want to win the spiritual battles that we face, we must develop a culture of faith, not a culture of fear.

Faith is the revelation of God's kingdom in the now; whenever faith is in operation, the power of God's kingdom is in manifestation. Recall that Jesus told His disciples, *"I give unto you power to tread on serpents and scorpions, and over all the power of the enemy: and nothing shall by any means hurt you"* (Luke 10:19). This is the authority we have in Christ Jesus, and it is activated by faith. You will never be able to exercise authority you don't believe you possess.

GOD HAS CALLED EVERY BELIEVER TO LIVE A LIFE OF FAITH RATHER THAN A LIFE OF FEAR.

Contrary to popular belief, fear is not the absence of faith—it is faith in reverse. Whenever we are operating in fear, it is because we have believed something that is false. Imagine going to your doctor for a test and waiting in the examination room for him or her to return, only to hear the words, "This looks very interesting!" Immediately, you think, *Something is wrong!* The moment this anxious thought is entertained, the mind becomes seized with anxiety. This is the definition of fear that I like to use: false, misleading, or exaggerated evidence appearing real.

The only way to overcome the temptation to fear is by faith in the Word of God. Instead of jumping to the worst conclusion possible, we ought to declare God's Word as the final authority in every matter. Faith says, "Everything is going to be fine, because the Lord is my Helper!" We must hold up the shield of faith in order to protect ourselves against the spirit of fear.

The Bible tells us, **"*There is no fear in love; but perfect love casteth out fear: because fear hath torment. He that feareth is not made perfect in love*"** (1 John 4:18). The word "*fear*" in this passage comes from the Greek word *phobos*, which means "terror." This term gives us our English word *phobia*—"an extreme or irrational fear of or aversion to something." This fear is experienced when we allow the enemy to manipulate the circumstances of our lives and distort our reality. And this kind of fear can alienate us from the life that God intended us to live—a life of faith and victory. *"For whatsoever is born of God overcometh the world: and this is the victory that overcometh the world,* **even our faith**" (1 John 5:4).

Taking Dominion Over Fear

Now that we know the importance of walking by faith, we can begin to exercise dominion over the spirit of fear. One day, I was praying in my room with the lights off when I sensed that someone was standing behind me. This was deeply disturbing, for, you see, when I was a young boy, my family would often watch horror movies. In fact, I can remember being forced to watch frightening movies as a child. These films deposited a seed of fear deep within my soul. As a result, every time I found myself alone in a room, as I often do when intending to pray, I would experience a subtle fear in the back of my mind that I was being watched or that some unwelcome guest was present in the room with me.

Finally, one day, I decided that enough was enough. I couldn't stand the feeling of being afraid any longer; therefore, I yelled out with a loud voice, "Devil, I am not afraid of you! You can't harm me, in the name of Jesus Christ!" To be honest with you, I didn't fully understand what I was doing at the time. Now I know: I was holding up the shield of faith and quenching the fiery darts of fear and terror. I have not lived in fear since then. Hallelujah!

The Bible says, *"God hath not given us the spirit of fear; but of power, and of love, and of a sound mind"* (2 Timothy 1:7). The word *"fear"* in this particular passage is not *phobia* but rather comes from the Greek word *deilia*, which refers to "timidity" or cowardice. In other words, God has not given us the spirit of cowardice but one of supernatural love, supernatural power, and supernatural soundness of mind. When you recognize that the spirit of fear does not come from God, you can resist it with all of your being.

We must refuse to be afraid! The power of the Holy Spirit working in and through us makes us bold and tenacious, in Jesus' name.

GOD HAS CALLED US TO CONQUER EVERY AREA OF FEAR IN OUR LIVES THROUGH THE POWER OF THE HOLY SPIRIT.

In the Psalm 27, David uttered these profound words: *"The Lord is my light and my salvation; whom shall I fear? the Lord is the strength of my life; of whom shall I be afraid?"* (Psalm 27:1). Do you realize that the Lord is your light and salvation? David realized that God was his light and salvation; as a result, he was able to overcome his fears.

You have no need to fear anymore! Why? Because God is your source of divine protection. He is your Deliverer! Though this may seem very obvious to some, you would be surprised at how many people are ignorant of this spiritual truth. One of the reasons for this widespread ignorance is the fact that we live in a society that is inundated with fear and dread. Every time we turn on the television or go online, the media barrages us with reports designed to provoke fear and anxiety.

Before we can resist this demonic assault, we first must recognize that fear is a spirit. We mentioned earlier that we can't take authority over something that we fear. This is because the spirit of fear paralyzes its victims. We cannot be in faith and in fear simultaneously. Every time we surrender to the spirit of fear, we weaken the integrity of our spiritual armor. On the other hand, every time we refuse to yield to the influence of fear in our lives, our spiritual armor is fortified.

Have you ever entertained the notion of a life without fear? Do you ever long to go to sleep without experiencing a single nightmare? Well, not only is this possible, but it is the absolute will of God. He has purposed and ordained a life completely devoid of fear. All you have to do is believe the Word of God. The moment you believe, the power of fear is broken, once and for all!

Revelation Changes Everything

One day, while I was driving down the street, the Holy Spirit asked me a profound question. He said, "Kynan, what is revelation?" Initially, this question struck me as very simple and elementary. However, the more I thought about it, I came to realize that it was one of the most important questions the Lord could have asked me.

"Revelation is an unveiling of something you didn't know before!" I finally exclaimed. Then the Holy Spirit asked me a second question: "How do you know when you have revelation?" This time, the Lord answered His own question in my spirit, saying, "WHEN EVERYTHING CHANGES!"

Most people probably think of a revelation as a moment of enlightenment or a fuzzy feeling in our stomach, but those things have nothing to do with revelation. The way that we can assuredly know that we have authentic revelation is by the manifestation that it produces. Revelation *always* produces manifestation. If it doesn't produce change in your life, it's not revelation; it's mental assent.

Let's use 1 Peter 2:24 as an example. It says, "[Jesus] *his own self bare our sins in his own body on the tree, that we, being dead to sins, should live unto righteousness: by whose stripes ye were healed*" (1 Peter 2:24). Once you have a revelation from God about this spiritual truth, it will permanently alter the way you respond to sickness and disease. This is why revelation is so important!

FAITH BRINGS THE REVELATION TO OUR INNER BEING THAT WE NEED TO OVERCOME THE ATTACKS OF THE EVIL ONE.

This is why the Bible says, *"Without faith it is impossible to please him"* (Hebrews 11:6)—because faith reveals the nature and power of God in every circumstance we encounter. Without knowing who God is (by faith), it would be impossible for us to truly worship Him. The same stands true of spiritual warfare. Without having a revelation of God's Word in our lives, it would be impossible to successfully resist the enemy.

Revelation changes everything! The moment I received a revelation by the Holy Spirit that I no longer needed to be afraid of the devil, faith came alive in my spirit, and fear had to bow to it. Until you receive revelation, your affirmations and confessions will be empty and powerless. You will scream idle words, and the devil won't budge. But once you have a revelation from God regarding His Word, shedding light on who God is and who you are, the devil will run screaming out the back door of your life. I am a living witness to the power and importance of having revelatory faith.

Deliverance Prayer

Father, in the name of Jesus, I thank You for who You are and for all that You have done. Right now, in the name of Jesus, I declare that I have great faith. I have the "God kind of faith" described in Mark 11:22–23, and every mountain in my life and in the lives of those around me must obey my voice. I open my mouth right now and say that all traces of doubt and unbelief must go from me. I am a believer of the Word of God. Every word in the Bible is the truth, and I believe it. The Word of God is the final authority in my life. I am not moved by what I see, think, or feel; I am moved only by the Word of God. I walk by faith in the Word of God and not by sight. I am not controlled by my emotions, others' emotions, or my environment, but I am completely dominated by God's Word.

Romans 10:17 declares that faith comes by hearing, and hearing by the Word of God. I am a hearer of Your Word, and, as a result, I have faith. Faith is the revelation of God's Word in action; therefore, I am a doer of Your Word. Nothing is impossible for me, because I am a believer of Your Word. Right now, I take authority over the spirit of fear, dread, doubt, and apprehension. I declare that I possess the mind of Christ and that I have not received a spirit of bondage to fear, but one of power, love, and soundness of mind. In Jesus' name, amen!

STAND AND FIGHT!

Watch ye, stand fast in the faith, quit you like men, be strong.
—1 Corinthians 16:13

The Bible gives us this prophetic picture of the birth of Jesus in the book of Isaiah:

> *For unto us a child is born, unto us a son is given: and the government shall be upon his shoulder: and his name shall be called Wonderful, Counsellor, The mighty God, The everlasting Father, The Prince of Peace.* (Isaiah 9:6)

The word *"government"* comes from the Hebrew word *misrah*, which refers to an empire or dominion. This prophetic verse of Scripture offers a description of our wonderful Messiah, the Lord Jesus.

The prophet Isaiah declares that *"the government shall be upon his shoulder."* In Hebrew, the word *"shoulder,"* *shĕkem*, refers to the shoulder blade or back. The implication is that the Messiah would not only carry the entire weight of the nation of Israel but also bear the rule and dominion of God upon his shoulders. The last time I checked, the shoulder blade was part of the body! And who is the body of Christ? We are! *"Now ye are the body of Christ, and members in particular"* (1 Corinthians 12:27). We are His body, and, as such, we have been given rule and dominion in the earth to advance the kingdom of God and demolish the kingdom of darkness.

What are you waiting for? Paul admonishes the church to *"watch, stand fast in the faith, quit you like men, be strong."* The term *"stand fast"* comes from the Greek word *stēkō*, which means "to persevere." This is what God has called us to do. He wants us to stand our ground and not give in to the onslaughts of Satan.

WE CARRY THE RULE AND GOVERNMENT OF GOD WITH US EVERYWHERE WE GO. THEREFORE, WE NEVER HAVE TO SURRENDER TO THE ENEMY AGAIN.

Why does Paul tell the church to stand fast? He knows that there is a temptation to give up. All of us have, at one time or another, entertained the thought of quitting. But this is not the will of God. "Stand fast" is a military expression, and we know that we are engaged in a spiritual war. The amazing news is that the enemy of our soul has been defeated. How sad would it be for us lose to a defeated foe? The reason I wrote this book is because there are millions of people all over the world who don't know that they already have the victory.

As we have mentioned before, spiritual warfare is all about positioning. When the Bible commands us to stand fast, it is calling us to assume a position of faith and confidence in God's Word, knowing that He cannot fail. In other words, we must be sure-footed and bold in God. We cannot be spiritual cowards or deserters. I don't know about you, but I refuse to allow the enemy to take another inch of my life. I want it all back! Every promise that he has thwarted, every blessing he has stolen (or I have surrendered to him), I want back—now!

What about you? Are you willing to fight for your promises? Your blessings? Your freedom? You can't really appreciate the value of freedom until you have been bound. I have been bound before, and I can tell you that it is not a good situation to be in. I refuse to be bound again, in Jesus' name!

The next thing that the apostle Paul tells us to do in 1 Corinthians 16:13 is to *"be strong."* This command comes from the Greek word *krataioō*, which means "to…increase in vigor; wax strong." Simply put, God is in the business of empowerment. Every promise in the Word of God is designed to strengthen us in our inner man.

Fighting for Your Prophetic Promises

We will never be able to live the abundant life that God has ordained for us if we are unwilling to fight. By fight, I do not mean physically but spiritually. Remember, the Bible says that the weapons of our warfare are not carnal, but mighty through God to the pulling down of strongholds. (See 2 Corinthians 10:4.) God has made awesome promises to His people. These promises are so magnanimous that they are beyond human reasoning and comprehension. The Bible says, *"Eye hath not seen, nor ear heard, neither have entered into the heart of man, the things which God hath prepared for them that love him"* (1 Corinthians 2:9).

I am reminded of the prophet Daniel, who wrote the following:

> In the first year of his reign I Daniel understood by books the number of the years, whereof the word of the LORD came to Jeremiah the prophet, that he would accomplish seventy years in the desolations of Jerusalem. (Daniel 9:2)

During the time in history described in the book of Daniel, the Israelites had been enslaved to the Babylonian Empire for over seventy years. Daniel realized from reading the scroll that the years of their captivity, as foretold by the prophet Jeremiah, had been fulfilled. In fact, by this time, the Israelites' time in Babylon had long expired. What was the problem? Why were they still in captivity if God had said they would remain in Babylon for only seventy years? Someone needed to rise up and insist upon seeing the prophetic promises of God fulfilled.

UNTIL WE PLACE A DEMAND ON THE WORD OF GOD, NOTHING IN OUR LIVES WILL CHANGE.

Once Daniel received this revelation, he went before the Lord with prayer and fasting. It seems that in today's society, the church doesn't emphasize prayer and fasting as much as it should. We somehow believe that fasting is old-fashioned and legalistic, but this belief is nothing more than a scheme of the enemy to keep us in bondage.

The Bible says that Daniel prayed and set his face unto the Lord. (See Daniel 9:3.) Prayer and fasting are a powerful means of releasing supernatural breakthrough in your life. Daniel understood this spiritual principle, and he sought the Lord with his whole heart.

If you want to experience true, lasting change in your life, you must seek the Lord with your entire being. There is a myth in the body of Christ that suggests the promises of God will come to pass through osmosis. In other words, many people think that God's promises will take place automatically. Nothing could be further from the truth. The prophetic promises and blessings of God are enjoyed when you and I place a demand on those promises.

The moment Daniel prayed, things began to move supernaturally.

> And whiles I was speaking, and praying, and confessing my sin and the sin of my people Israel, and presenting my supplication before the LORD my God for the holy mountain of my God; yea, whiles I was speaking in prayer, even the man Gabriel, whom I had seen in the vision at the beginning, being caused to fly swiftly, touched me about the time of the evening oblation. (Daniel 9:20–21)

Daniel received an angelic visitation the moment he made the decision to move beyond his comfort zone and press into the promises of God by faith. The moment you press beyond your feelings and emotions in order to engage God in prayer is the moment you will begin experiencing the supernatural turnaround that you have long anticipated.

The Spirit of Prevention

The tenth chapter of Daniel records that Daniel engaged in fasting and prayer for three full weeks; at the end of this time, he received a divine visitation. There appeared to Daniel a man in fine linen, his feet like polished brass.

> Then said he unto me, Fear not, Daniel: for from the first day that thou didst set thine heart to understand, and to chasten thyself before thy God, thy words were heard, and I am come for thy words. But the prince of the kingdom of Persia withstood me one and twenty days: but, lo, Michael, one of the chief princes, came to help me; and I remained there with the kings of Persia. (Daniel 10:12–13)

If you notice, the heavenly being who revealed himself to Daniel told him that his prayer was heard from the very first day, but that while he was en route to reach Daniel with the answer to his prayer, the prince of the Kingdom of Persia withstood him. Who is this prince? In the context of this particular passage of Scripture, it was a demonic principality assigned to the region of Persia. This demonic principality was responsible for hindering or preventing prayers from being answered. This is what we call a "spirit of prevention"—a demonic force that seeks to hinder the manifestation of prayers, prophecies, breakthroughs, and progress in the life of believers. If you have ever felt strong spiritual opposition when you were doing something God called you to do, it was because the spirit of prevention was interfering.

THE SPIRIT OF PREVENTION TRIES TO DISCOURAGE BELIEVERS BY HINDERING THE PROMISES OF GOD FROM MANIFESTING IN THEIR LIVES.

Many years ago, our ministry was not growing or experiencing the blessings and provision that we knew God had ordained for us. As I began to pray and fast, the Holy Spirit revealed to me that we were dealing with a spirit of prevention. I asked the Lord what I should do about it, and the Lord spoke to me and said, "You must do what I did in the beginning of creation! When there was void and darkness, I spoke the Word to it and commanded the light to come forth."

So, one day while praying, I decided to take authority over this hindering spirit and declare the promises of God's Word over our ministry. I said, "In the name of Jesus Christ, light be!" The hindering spirit was lifted immediately. Several weeks later, we began to notice growth and increase in our church like never before. Even the financial giving in our ministry began to increase exponentially. How did this happen? We addressed the spiritual forces that were preventing our ministry from realizing its full potential.

You can do the same thing in your life. Once you recognize what God has promised you, take a stand and fight for those promises, in Jesus' name. What has the devil hindered in your life? Is it financial prosperity? Career success? A thriving ministry? You must take authority over the spirit of prevention right now! Too many believers are sitting around waiting for something to happen while they suffer unnecessarily. This is nothing more than a device of the enemy. Lay hold of God's promises now!

Knowing Your Enemy's Playbook

When I was younger, I was heavily involved in sports. One common practice among sports coaches is to familiarize themselves with the opposing team's playbook before a game or match. A playbook is simply a manual cataloging a sports team's strategies and plays.

Just like sports teams in the natural, Satan also has a playbook that he carefully follows when engaging in spiritual attacks against God's people. The sooner you familiarize yourself with the devil's playbook, the sooner you can uncover his demonic strategies.

As we mentioned previously, there are three main objectives of the enemy: fear, intimidation, and control. Every demonic attack on a believer originates from one of these three areas. Oftentimes, football players will spend hours on end studying the plays of the opposing team. By doing so, they are positioning themselves to have a strategic advantage during game time.

The Word of God unveils the playbook of the devil. In the book of 2 Kings, the Bible records that the King of Syria waged war against Israel and took counsel with his servants to encamp in a certain location.

> And the man of God sent unto the king of Israel, saying, Beware that thou pass not such a place; for thither the Syrians are come down. And the king of Israel sent to the place which the man of God told him and warned him of, and saved himself there, not once nor twice. (2 Kings 6:9–10)

Simply put, God revealed the plans of the enemy ahead of time; as a result, the life of the King of Israel was preserved three times.

GOD REVEALS THE TACTICS AND STRATEGIES OF THE ENEMY BEFOREHAND BY THE HOLY SPIRIT AND THE REVEALED WORD OF GOD.

The Bible says, "*Whoso diggeth a pit shall fall therein: and he that rolleth a stone, it will return upon him*" (Proverbs 26:27). The more you meditate on the Word of God and pray in the Holy Spirit, the more the Lord will uncover the devices of the evil one in your life. This does not mean that you need to obsess about the attacks of the enemy, only that you ought to be diligent and vigilant when it comes to spiritual warfare.

I declare that the counsel of the devil is confused, in Jesus' name. I declare that no weapon formed against you shall prosper!

One night, I had a dream that we were having a church service that was very powerful. While the service was going on, I noticed that there was also a commotion outside the church building. When I stepped outside, there were snakes on the walkway leading into the church. These snakes were preventing people from coming inside. I took a machete and began cutting the serpents into pieces, and then I awoke from my dream. Once I shared the details of my dream with my wife, it dawned on me that this was a prophetic warning by the Holy Spirit. It turns out that God was exposing demonic activity—in this case, witchcraft—within our church. We soon discovered that someone with a slanderous spirit was attempting to deter people from joining our church. A few weeks later, the person involved in this demonic activity was exposed and dealt with appropriately.

I share this story with you to illustrate the importance of exposing the enemy's tactics. No longer will the devil take you by surprise. The devil's *modus operandi* has not changed one iota since the beginning of time. His agenda is to kill, steal, and destroy. The good news is that our Father's agenda is to save, heal, and restore!

Arise and Shine!

In the book of Isaiah, the prophet says, *"Arise, shine; for thy light is come, and the glory of the* LORD *is risen upon thee"* (Isaiah 60:1). The word *"arise"* comes from the Hebrew word *quwm*, which means "stand (up)." I believe that God is releasing a clarion call to His church to stand up and fulfill her destiny. It is time for the saints to take their places in the kingdom of God.

Isaiah 60:1 says that our light has come, and the glory of the Lord has risen upon us! Jesus said, *"Let your light so shine before men, that they may see your good works, and glorify your Father which is in heaven"* (Matthew 5:16). We are the light of the world, and the universe is waiting for the children of God to manifest the light of heaven in the earth. Everything that we have discussed thus far has been meant to encourage you. God has called, equipped, and empowered us to take His kingdom to every corner of the earth. He wants us to release the culture of heaven everywhere we go. It is time for the body of Christ to rise up and take dominion over the powers of darkness. No longer will we allow Satan to buffet us while we behave like victims. No longer will we allow addiction, depression, and fear to torment us. Stand up, in Jesus' name! The glory of God has already been revealed in and through you. Are you tired of being confined by life-controlling issues? Are you tired of being oppressed by the enemy of your soul? I declare that today is the day of your freedom!

GOD HAS CHOSEN YOU TO BE A LIGHT TO THE NATIONS AND TO MANIFEST HIS POWER AND GLORY.

The moment we became born again, we were grafted into God's kingdom as sons and daughters. We were given the full rights and privileges of the citizens of the kingdom of heaven. It doesn't matter where you are today—you may be feeling confined to a prison of hopelessness or a pit of perversion—but God's Word will never return void. (See Isaiah 55:11.) You can experience true and lasting freedom in your life. What He has purposed and promised you will surely come to pass. No demon in hell can stop the freedom that God has given you from manifesting in your life. However, you must fight for it!

The biggest deception that the enemy can conjure is the lie that says, "You will never break free from this addiction. Your life will never change!" The devil is a liar! Not only can you break free, but you *will* break free! If the Son (Jesus Christ) has made you free, then you shall be free indeed. (See John 8:36.)

My prayer is that, through reading this book and applying the principles herein, you will be empowered to walk in the purpose and destiny that God has ordained for your life. We are in the greatest time in human history, and the Bible says that the glory of the latter house shall be greater than the former. (See Haggai 2:9.) We are the generation that will experience the power and presence of God like none before us. We are the generation that will take dominion over all the powers of darkness and live out the true intent of Luke 10:19. May the Lord bless you and keep you, in Jesus' name!

Deliverance Prayer

Father, in Jesus' name, I take authority over the forces of darkness. The Word of God declares in Luke 10:19, "*Behold, I give unto you power to tread on serpents and scorpions, and over all the power of the enemy: and nothing shall by any means hurt you.*" I know that I have power and authority over the evil one, and that nothing he says, does, or suggests will bring harm to myself or to anyone in my family.

I now expose my entire spirit, soul, and body to the Word of God, the fire of the Holy Spirit, and the blood of Jesus Christ; I command any spirit, force, influence, or agency operating illegally in my soul to cease and desist and to be uprooted by the power of the blood of Jesus Christ. I pull down any and all demonic strongholds, in Jesus' name, and I cast down all wicked imaginations that would seek to contradict the authority and truth of the Word of God.

I confess that I am clean through the Word, according to John 15:3 and Ephesians 5:26. My body is the temple of the Holy Spirit, according to 1 Corinthians 6:19; as a result, the only spirit that has permission to occupy my temple is the Holy Spirit. Today, I declare that all demonic oppression must cease from this day forward. I walk in kingdom authority and dominion over all the powers of darkness, and I am free to worship the Lord without fear, guilt, or shame, in Jesus' name. Amen!

ABOUT THE AUTHOR

Dr. Kynan T. Bridges is the senior pastor of Grace & Peace Global Fellowship in Tampa, Florida. With a profound revelation of the Word of God and a dynamic teaching ministry, Dr. Bridges has revolutionized the lives of many in the body of Christ. Through his practical approach to applying the deep truths of the Word of God, he reveals the authority and identity of the new covenant believer.

God has placed on Dr. Bridges a particular anointing for understanding and teaching the Scriptures, along with the gifts of prophecy and healing. Dr. Bridges and his wife, Gloria, through an apostolic anointing, are committed to equipping the body of Christ to live in the supernatural every day and to fulfill the Great Commission. It is Dr. Bridges's desire to see the nations transformed by the unconditional love of God.

A highly sought speaker and published author of a number of books, his previous books with Whitaker House include *Unlocking the Code of the Supernatural*, *School of the Miraculous*, *Invading the Heavens*, *Unmasking the Accuser*, *The Power of Prophetic Prayer*, and *Kingdom Authority*. Dr. Bridges is a committed husband, a mentor, and a father of five beautiful children: Ella, Naomi, Isaac, Israel, and Anna.

Welcome to Our House!

We Have a Special Gift for You

It is our privilege and pleasure to share in your love of Christian books. We are committed to bringing you authors and books that feed, challenge, and enrich your faith.

To show our appreciation, we invite you to sign up to receive a specially selected **Reader Appreciation Gift**, with our compliments. Just go to the Web address at the bottom of this page.

God bless you as you seek a deeper walk with Him!

WE HAVE A GIFT FOR YOU. VISIT:

whpub.me/nonfictionthx

WHITAKER HOUSE